Gardening
IN SPAIN

Marcelle Pitt

SANTANA
BOOKS

Published by Ediciones Santana, S.L. in March 1997

First published in September 1988

Revised and expanded edition in November 1991

Illustrations by Heber Clewett

Photography by AGE Fotostock, Barcelona; Wayne Chasan, and Jean-Dominique Dallet

Published by Ediciones Santana, S.L.
Apartado 422, 29640 Fuengirola (Málaga), Spain

Printed in Spain. Imprime: Gráficas SAN PANCRACIO, S.L., Pol. Ind. San Luis, C/. La Orotava, 17, Málaga

Depósito Legal: MA-312/1997 - ISBN: 84-921229-8-6

To Jack

With grateful thanks to the many friends who have
shared their gardens and their expertise with me.

CONTENTS

SPAIN —
The Gardener's Dream

ALL of us who love gardening — and even people who have never gardened before — feel at once on coming to live in Spain that it is a chance of gardening in paradise.

The brilliant light, a welcoming climate, and the flowers, trees and shrubs growing everywhere, all combine to tempt us to try to grow something ourselves.

Of course there is a winter season. Rain must fall. But coming as we did from Northumberland in the north-east of England, it seemed unbelievable that in this subtropical climate, the sun shines all the year round.

Where was the snow, the ice, the freezing wind and the low, grey sky pressing down for a fortnight at a time?

In midwinter in our northern garden the high beeches would be bare. Little voles would be running through their domed tunnels under the snow. The hedgehog would be sleeping the winter away deep in the Irish yew. Here we had come to live in an unbelievable world of good weather, colour and sunshine.

One neighbour said: "You never get bad weather all day here. If it rains in the morning, the sun comes out in the afternoon."

Perhaps that isn't strictly true. You may get some steady rain. We have one or two storms most winters when the rain dances in sideways from the bay in squalls, looking like a regiment of ghosts storming the sand-dunes.

But the rain never lasts long. The trees in the garden are green. The terrace is bright with geraniums. Outside one set of flowers hands over to another, like runners in a relay race.

White showers of December jasmine and flaming aloes cheer the garden. Fluffy yellow mimosa gives scent and colour together. The fuchsias, Christmas cacti and poinsettias of December lead straight on to the pink flowering cherry, narcissi, hazel catkins, bougainvillaea, heather and lemons of January.

In case I have been carried away with enthusiasm as I write, I have checked my diary. We have flowers in borders, on bushes, trees or on the patio every day of the year.

Naturally, gardening in Spain is different from gardening in colder climates. Look round and see what grows well in your area before you set about it. Everyone is prepared to help you.

Whether you live in a palace or an apartment, whether you plan to lay out rich acres or content yourself with bright pots on a balcony. Spain is the fulfilment of a gardener's dream.

Climate

HE climate of the Spanish kingdom varies greatly, from the high peaks of the Pyrenees in the north, to the furthest sunbaked promontories of the Canary Islands lying off the coast of Africa. But for the practical purposes of this book — for gardens are made where people choose to live — I have narrowed the information on climate to nine areas: the eight most popular regions for foreigners, and also Madrid.

Madrid, though extreme in climate on its high central plateau, is yet such a magnetic capital city that some foreigners will always live there, and wish to surround their homes with plants and flowers. For the rest, each of the Costa or Island areas of Spain has its own particular charms and devotees. This applies also to regions inland where the Arabs liked

CLIMATE
Average Temperatures in Fahrenheit and Celsius, and Rainfall in Inches as supplied by the Spanish Meteorological Office in 1990

		Jan		Feb		Mar		Abr		May	
		°F	°C	°F	°C	°F	°C	°F	°C	°F	°C
COSTA BRAVA (Cape Bagur)											
Temp.	Max	57	14	57	14	61	16	63	17	68	20
	Min	43	6	43	6	46	8	49	9	55	13
Rainfall		1.4		1.7		3.4		2.3		2.5	
COSTA DORADA (Barcelona)											
Temp.	Max	56	13	58	14	61	16	65	18	70	21
	Min	43	6	45	7	49	9	52	11	58	14
Rainfall		1.3		1.6		1.8		1.8		2.0	
COSTA DEL AZAHAR (Valencia)											
Temp.	Max	59	15	61	16	65	18	68	20	74	23
	Min	43	6	43	6	47	8	50	10	56	13
Rainfall		1.3		1.2		1.1		1.3		1.2	
COSTA BLANCA (Alicante)											
Temp.	Max	61	16	63	17	68	20	72	22	78	26
	Min	44	7	43	6	47	8	50	10	56	13
Rainfall		1.3		0.8		0.7		1.6		1.1	
COSTA DEL SOL (Málaga)											
Temp.	Max	63	17	63	17	67	19	70	21	74	23
	Min	49	9	49	9	52	11	56	13	59	15
Rainfall		2.3		1.9		2.4		1.8		1.0	
COSTA DE LA LUZ (Cádiz)											
Temp.	Max	59	15	58	14	65	18	70	21	74	23
	Min	47	8	45	7	52	11	54	12	59	15
Rainfall		2.8		2.2		3.1		1.7		1.2	
CASTILLA (Madrid)											
Temp.	Max	49	9	52	11	59	15	65	18	70	21
	Min	34	1	36	2	41	5	54	12	50	10
Rainfall		1.5		1.3		1.8		1.8		1.7	
BALEARES (Mallorca)											
Temp. Max		58	14	59	15	63	17	67	19	72	22
	Min	43	6	43	6	47	8	50	10	56	12
Rainfall		1.5		1.3		1.4		1.1		1.0	
CANARIAS (Tenerife)											
Temp.	Max	68	20	70	21	72	22	74	23	76	24
	Min	58	14	58	14	59	15	61	16	63	17
Rainfall		1.4		1.5		1.0		0.5		0.2	

June		July		Aug		Sept		Oct		Nov		Dec	
°F	°C	°F	°C	°F	°C	°F	°C	°F	°C	°F	°C	°F	°C
74	23	80	27	78	26	77	25	69	21	62	17	59	15
60	16	65	18	69	21	62	16	55	13	49	9	45	7
2.2		1.7		2.2		3.4		3.6		2.1		2.2	
77	25	83	28	83	28	77	25	70	21	61	16	56	13
65	18	70	21	70	21	66	19	59	15	52	11	47	8
1.7		1.1		1.5		3.0		3.2		1.9		1.5	
79	26	84	29	84	29	81	27	74	23	66	19	61	16
61	16	66	19	68	20	65	18	59	15	50	10	45	7
0.8		0.3		0.8		2.1		3.4		1.4		1.4	
84	29	90	32	90	32	86	30	77	25	70	21	63	17
61	16	66	19	68	20	65	18	59	15	50	10	45	7
0.5		0.1		0.5		1.8		2.2		1.3		1.1	
81	27	84	29	86	30	84	29	74	23	68	20	63	17
66	19	70	21	72	22	68	20	61	16	54	12	49	9
0.2		0		0.1		1.1		2.4		2.5		2.6	
81	27	84	29	86	30	84	29	74	23	68	20	63	17
65	18	68	20	68	20	66	19	59	15	54	12	49	9
0.2		0		0.1		1.0		2.8		3.1		2.7	
81	27	88	31	86	30	77	25	66	19	56	13	49	9
58	14	63	17	63	17	58	14	50	10	41	5	36	2
1.0		0.4		0.5		1.2		2.1		1.8		1.9	
79	26	84	29	84	29	81	27	74	23	65	18	59	15
63	17	66	19	68	20	65	18	58	14	50	10	47	8
0.8		0.1		0.9		2.2		3.0		3.6		3.0	
79	26	83	28	84	29	83	28	79	26	75	24	70	21
66	19	68	20	70	21	70	21	66	19	63	17	61	16
0		0		0		0.1		1.2		1.8		2.0	

to live and where other discerning *extranjeros* have followed.

Climate varies not only with latitude but also with altitude, the height above sea-level. In Catalonia for instance, the vines are planted along the coast and at varying heights, racing up the hillsides in a few kilometres to 2,000 feet and what is known as the "potato line", where grapes give way to vegetables. A climate to suit many tastes lies in the variations between.

The Costa Blanca has been described by the World Health Organization as having "almost as perfect an environment as it is possible to obtain", with its hot summers and mild winters.

The Costa del Sol is the most popular region of all among Spain's new residents — again with hot summers, mild winters and a superb climate for flowers.

Whether you live west on the Costa de la Luz, with its fertile charm and Atlantic breezes, or east in the Balearic Islands of the Mediterranean — another of the many favoured regions — or choose to go south to Gran Canaria where strawberries begin at Christmas, there are many fine climates for life and leisure, and above all for gardeners.

I am grateful to the Spanish Meteorological Office for the foregoing tables supplied in 1990 as an indication of temperature and rainfall in various regions.

Planning Your Garden

ONLY those who live in Spain realize how much time is spent out of doors.

Your garden assumes an even greater importance, because here the subtropical climate brings colour and fragrance every month of the year. Spain is truly the country of the garden.

Every plot is different and every garden will finally be as individual as its owner. You may be faced with a completely uncultivated area, or take over an existing garden which is not quite what you want.

In all circumstances there are certain points to bear in mind. You may decide for them or against them, but the very fact that you have considered these matters will help you to decide what you really want.

The Step-by-Step Approach

Stand with your back to the house and look over the land. Arrange for an open space next to the house. This will give a feeling of light and freedom.

If possible, plan so that you can't see all the garden at once. A clump of flowering shrubs, or trees perhaps, lend an air of interest and mystery. At first sight, who knows what lies beyond? Arrange for a terrace to link home and garden. It makes an ideal place to sit, and at the same time protects the foundations of the house from the water that the grass will need.

In a small garden, soften the all-too-visible boundaries. A hedge instead of a wall avoids that "don't fence me in" feeling. Think of privacy. In a large garden this may cause no problem, but you might like to plant a hedge or bushes to screen the tennis court from the approach to the front door for instance, or there may be a distant eyesore such as a tall block of flats that can easily be masked by a strategically placed and quick-growing tree. Sometimes an attractive, distant view is brought more sharply into focus by a frame of foliage.

In a smaller garden, privacy is of even greater importance. A trellis attached to the fence and covered with quick-growing climbers can provide a floral screen. If the garden is near a busy road, edge it with trees. Very many trees in Spain keep their leaves all the year, and cut out a surprising amount of dust and glare.

Plan your paths to see that they go where you need them. Unless you wish for rigidly classical lines, you may want to curve your paths rather than make them ruler straight. As the artists say: "Curved is the line of beauty." If it seems naturally right in the circumstances that a path should be straight, the effect can be softened by flowers growing nearby.

Springtime in a Spanish garden. (Photo by J. D. D.)

Bright yellow, long-flowering Lantana, backed by a clump of Pampas-Grass and the strawberry tree (Arbutus), in a Mediterranean garden. Bougainvillaea graces the wall. (Photo by J. D. D.)

If the ground slopes away from the house, put bright bushes rather than a low flower bed in the distance. They can be seen the moment you enter the garden.

In a new garden, decide whether you would like to put down an infrastructure of underground water pipes before you make the lawn. Whether it is to be a sophisticated drip system of underground irrigation or a simpler system of water pipes to service a hose and sprinklers, do it now.

Finally plan storage for your equipment. A mower and tools to give of their best must have a fit place to live.

Soil

Most gardens in Spain have good soil. Take care to keep it good and to improve it where necessary.

Occasionally villas are built on beautiful hillsides where the soil is inadequate for producing fine flowers. In this case, buy soil from a local nursery garden or, in a small area, make a garden entirely in planters filled with any mixture you need.

When budgeting for your garden, place farm manure high on your list of priorities. It is not cheap, but can be obtained from nursery gardens, and is more worthwhile than many showy garden luxuries.

Farm manure not only feeds plants but alters the nature of the soil, making it not only richer, but also more open and friable and so more easily penetrated by growing roots. Never use farm manure until it is well rotted. It increases the actual bulk of the soil, unlike chemical fertilizers which nourish and stimulate plants without altering the texture of the earth.

Compost

Save fallen leaves, lawn cuttings (except for the first cutting after the application of weed-killer) and all soft garden refuse to enrich the land that grew them.

There are many schools of thought as to how best to treat this waste vegetable matter, but all agree that both moisture and air are needed to make good compost.

Some gardeners buy special bins with air inlets in the sides. These, with the use of a proprietary accelerator are probably the fastest way of getting the desired result.

Others erect a circular bin of wire netting and fill it with their garden refuse. Others — and often the most experienced — dig a shallow hole in the ground, a little under a metre in diameter, then build up their compost heap until it stands half a metre high or a little more, seeing that it is always damp. When one heap is built, another is started, and so on, according to the produce of the garden. This is not the quickest, but certainly an easy way of making good humus. With or without chemical additives, good, rich compost is produced in a year, and in far less time a rich, treacly-brown mulch is available which is excellent for helping plants and suppressing weeds in herbacious borders.

Never put thick, woody stems or virulent weeds on to the compost heap. It is better to burn them.

What Does My Soil Need?
Some Simple Tests To Assess Your Land

Good soil is one of the basic requirements of successful gardening. If in doubt as to the nature of the soil in your garden, make a few simple tests. Armed with the knowledge you gain you will know how to care for your plants.

Test for Texture
Take up a handful of earth, or turn over a forkful, and see if the soil is light and crumbly. If it is, roots of plants will penetrate easily, air can enter the earth and sustain the myriad unseen organisms which make up healthy soil. If the soil is hard when dry, and sticky when wet — clay soil — work to get the texture right. Suggestions follow.

Test for Good Drainage and Good Water Retention
Look at the land after heavy rain, or dig a hole and fill it with water. After an hour, if water is still lying in puddles on the surface of the soil, or the hole isn't empty, the drainage is badly deficient.

To treat heavy soil, dig in as much organic material (compost, ground bark, well-rotted manure, coconut fibre or peat) up to 50 per cent of the total volume of each flower bed. In extreme cases don't attempt to plant in the ground at all. Construct raised beds with good soil and good drainage, or use planters. Fortunately soil of this type is rare in Spain.

Perhaps your soil is sandy and water drains away extremely fast: again, add maximum quantities of organic material. This increases the ability of the soil to hold water.

Test for Acidity — the pH Factor

This measures whether soils can be classified as alkaline, neutral or acid. To test, an inexpensive meter is available for home gardeners. A pH of about 6.5 is ideal for general purposes.

Test for Chemicals

Soil test kits are also available, reasonably priced, which test not only for the pH factor but for the presence of other chemicals such as nitrogen and phosphorous. Clear instructions make the use of either of these aids easy.

Organic and Chemical Fertilizers

Land that produces good crops, whether flowers, fruit, vegetables or lawn grass, requires added nourishment to make up for what is continually taken away.

Organic fertilizers both nourish and also alter the texture of the soil. Chemical fertilizers don't affect the texture, but only the nutrients that the soil contains.

You may wish to give your garden a supply of both. If tests show special needs, buy a chemical fertilizer to balance the deficiencies. (Remember when reading labels that the ingredient contained in the largest amount comes first, and thereafter components are listed in decreasing order.)

The Tools for The Job

THE right tools make gardening easy, and a wide variety, both simple and sophisticated, can be bought in Spain.

Many gardeners — experts in their own countries — are uncertain how to set about getting the tools they need when they start to garden in Spain. Everything you need is available here. It is only necessary to know the Spanish name for what you want.

Go first to a good nursery garden, *vivero,* or a large store selling garden supplies. If they don't stock what you want themselves they will be able to tell you where to go. As large gardening items are expensive and take up a lot of room, many firms keep only a skeleton supply but will order what you want from catalogues.

Many larger items are imported, which means that the instructions are often printed in English and two or three other languages. When buying a capital item such as a lawn-mower, make sure that you can understand the service manual and also that back-up service facilities are available.

Some Useful Words

Dibber: *plantadora de punta;* makes holes for seedlings and large seeds.
Fork: *bielgo, bieldo.*
Hoe: *azadilla, escardillo;* comes in many types. One of the best is the Dutch hoe, which has the blade set in approximately the same plane as the handle and is used by pushing with a chopping movement. Another excellent model, the "Swoe" — made by a firm who formerly made swords — looks like a golf putter with a long handle and is sharp on both sides of the blade so that it can be worked both forwards and backwards. Light and strong, it covers ground rapidly without damaging plants.
Lawn-Mower (hand mower): *cortacésped manual.*
Long-Arm: *cortarramas de cuerda;* valuable for shaping trees without climbing a ladder.
Mattock: *azada, azadón.*
Pruning Knife: *podadera.*
Rake: *rastrillo;* removes stones and leaves, and smooths seed-beds.
Saw: *sierra;* it gave its name to the mountains with their saw-like outline.
Secateurs: *tijeras para podar;* buy a strong pair if you plan to deal with virile growers like bougainvillaea.
Shears: *tijeras de jardinero* (garden shears); *tijeras para setos* (hedging shears).
Sieve: *criba.*
Spade: *pala;* get one suited to your height and strength, and keep it sharp.
Trowel: *paleta, desplantador.*

Power-Driven Tools

Electric Grass Cutter: *cortacésped eléctrico;* a useful model is available (250 volt) which is light to use and good for difficult places, such as round a tree.
Electric Hedge Trimmer: *tijera eléctrica.*
Motor Mower: *cortacésped motor a gasolina autopropulsado.*
Rotary Cutter: *cortacésped rotativo;* useful for large areas of grass. A

good selection is available in Spain.

Other Useful Equipment

Axe: *hacha, segur.*

Basket: *cesta.*

Broom: *escoba.*

Flower Pots: *macetas.* Many sizes and varieties are available. Earthenware pots, being heavy, are less likely to fall over with tall plants. Plastic pots need less attention as they do not dry out through the sides and consequently need watering less often.

Greenhouse: *invernáculo, invernadero;* Spanish enthusiasts often erect a timber frame and line it annually with plastic. At the other end of the scale, lovers of exotic plants can buy highly sophisticated glasshouses which regulate heat, light and moisture by computer.

Hosepipe: *manguera.*

Ladder or Steps: *escalera;* bound to be needed sooner or later.

Seed Box: *semillero;* for the initial planting of small, valuable seeds.

Sprinkler: *rociador, aspersor.*

Watering Can: *regadera.* If you use weed-killer, have two cans and mark the deadly one clearly. (I once killed a greenhouseful of tomatoes by using the wrong one.)

Wheelbarrow: *carretilla;* choose a light one. You'll be glad you did.

Fertilizers and Peat

Manure: *estiércol.*

Fertilizer: *abono.*

Compound Fertilizer: *abono compuesto;* a useful mixture is called "Quince-Quince-Quince" taking its name from the fact that it contains 15 per cent nitrogen, 15 per cent phosphoric acid and 15 per cent potassium.

Peat: *turba.*

Concentrated Liquid Fertilizer: *fertilizante concentrado líquido;* excellent for potted plants.

Many other aids are available. No gardener in Spain need be hampered by lack of equipment.

Paths and Walkways

HAT makes a perfect path? First the obvious fact that it should go where you want it to go. From the terrace to the pool perhaps, from the door to the gazebo, or just through the dappled shade of an arbour to the olive tree on the wall.

Every garden is different, but each needs a network of good-looking and comfortable paths to supply the day-to-day needs and wishes of the owners.

Secondly, consider the question of walkability. A smooth, sloping path can be dangerous in wet weather, and cobbles, however, *típico,* are uncomfortable for high heels.

As to maintenance, this must be within the limits of the resources of time and money available.

Less obvious than the practical considerations, are those psychological effects produced by harmonious shades and subtle variations of texture and pattern in walkways. These are the "mood changers" of garden architecture, which subtly increase pleasure as you look at the plants.

The paths, terraces, steps and bridges where you walk will, if correctly chosen, add more to your sense of delight than you may realize.

When planning to put walkways through a garden, there is also the question of expense. A wide span of quality and workmanship is available, or you can decide to do it yourself. Once you decide what will be perfect for your garden, it is surprising how often intelligence can conjure the right effect from even a strict budget.

Practical Thoughts About Paths

The width of paths will vary according to the purpose for which they are needed. A path twisting up through a rockery may be no wider than 30 cm. To protect a beautiful lawn from wear, stepping stones 35 cm. square will be enough for occasional use. But in general, if space permits, paths should never be less than 60 cm. wide, and give a more gracious effect at 120 cm., or more.

Plan that any gradients should be easy; steps both look and feel good when wide and shallow. Never build steps with a rise of more than 17 cm.

On a flat site, charm the eye with variations of height. From time to time introduce a raised planter beside the walkways. Provide a masonry seat here and there. Cross a stream or narrow water garden with an arched wooden bridge, Japanese style. The variations of level will relax and delight the stroller, even if he is not fully aware of the cause of his pleasure.

Extremely fine examples of the pavior's art are to be found in Spain, and if expense is no object consult a top garden architect and work out your ideas with him. It may be expensive if the project is large, but you will be rewarded with a work of art which will last into the foreseeable future.

If your budget is moderate, state the limit clearly at your first meeting with your garden architect. These professionals can help you to get maximum value for money.

The Choice of Materials

Bricks and Pavers

First choose a dominant colour, perhaps a mellow honey-rose shade, which will look old when it is new and still fresh when it has grown old.

The bricks can be laid in a variety of patterns: herring-bone, L-shaped or in a simple, alternating wall fashion. Narrow bricks of the same shade laid end-on in bands 30 cm. wide can divide areas of differing patterns, adding a new dimension of texture.

On a clear space of brickwork lay out the points of the compass — magnificent in brass, or less expensive but still attractive with narrow bricks laid on edge in a contrasting colour. Either makes an interesting feature.

Try also 30-cm. square brick pavers in a complementary colour. Visitors will hardly notice the subtle changes of shapes and shades as they walk, yet subconsciously they will see the complex variations and feel that this garden is a place they are glad to be in.

Cobbles

Cobblestones set in concrete make attractive and durable paving. In some old village houses in Spain, where the donkey customarily lived downstairs and the family above, the small front courtyards are still paved with patterns of cobbles which have delighted — and been copied by — professional walkway architects in northen Europe.

A dramatic design uses black cobbles to pick out a pattern on white, or you can use other constrasting colours. But cobbles are tiring to walk on in their village state. Either raise the level of the concrete to make an easier walkway, or use cobbles laid traditionally on each side of a path constructed of smoother materials.

The use of cobblestones gives scope for individual choice and imagination. Cobbles made smooth by being deeply imbedded in concrete can also send another signal to the eye. Concrete can be coloured. Choose a sunny, sandy shade to indicate the central walkway, while embedding the rougher, rustic-set stones on each side of the path in an unnoticeable, darker mixture.

Sets

Granite paving stones known as sets were much used in the days of horse-drawn traffic as a surface which was easier to negotiate, but more expensive than cobbles. Today, architects in new developments in Spain have revived the use of these shallow-domed, brick-sized pavers in natural or reconstituted stone. Particularly attractive is the silver-grey variety.

Rectangular Paving

Genuine stone slabs are expensive but make dignified walkways and, being a natural substance, look particularly good with small plants growing among them. Reconstituted stone slabs are cheaper, although both are heavy enough in handling to be a difficult choice for the do-it-yourself gardener.

Bed stone slabs in sand to allow for levelling, or in concrete for a more durable path. If using concrete, be particularly careful to allow planting crevices right down to the soil beneath if you want small plants between the flagstones. Space paving stones no more than 2.5 cm. apart.

Crazy Paving

In Spain, crazy paving is a popular choice for informal paths. Bed the individual slabs in sand or concrete as for rectangular paving, since it is necessary to allow for irregularities of thickness. A spirit level is helpful to get an even, trouble-free path.

To estimate how much crazy paving stone is needed to cover a given area, examine the average thickness of the stones. Usually thickness varies from 1.5 cm. to 6 cm.

Paving stones 3-6 cm. thick are usually grouped together as thick crazy paving, and stones 1.5-3 cm. thick are sold as thin crazy paving. As a rule of thumb, 1,000 kg. of thick crazy paving will cover nine square metres and 1,000 kg. of thin crazy paving will cover 14 square metres.

Slate

Slate also makes an attractive and dignified walkway, although it may seem out of place in a truly rustic garden.

Gravel

Gravel makes a path that is easy on the eye, but it is important for satisfactory and lasting results to prepare the infrastructure carefully.

Gravel paths need a good foundation of hard material, such as broken brick, which must be consolidated into a firm base. The best gravel for paths is mixed with sand and clay to bind it into a smooth and lasting surface, and must be laid 7 cm. thick on the foundation.

Start with a slight camber in the centre to allow for easy drainage. Rake the gravel smooth, then roll it carefully, watering from time to time so that the gravel-clay-sand mixture becomes compacted and hard. A carefully-made gravel path lasts well and needs only occasional applications of weed-killer to keep it in good condition.

Concrete

Concrete paths are the cheapest and probably the easiest to manage for the amateur path-builder. Their rather plain surfaces can be improved almost out of recognition by mixing in colour to get a subtle shade and by the addition of a little gravel. This alleviates the blank look and texture and is a safety factor on sloping surfaces in wet weather.

When colouring concrete, mix a test sample first and allow it to dry fully, so that the final effect can be assessed.

As in all walkway construction, concrete should be spread on a hard rubble foundation. The mixture should be not less than 5 cm. thick.

When working with concrete it should dry slowly. This is essential. Try to avoid working in warm weather. If this is unavoidable, cover new concrete paths with damp sacking and keep it moist for at least a week. This allows the concrete to dry slowly underneath.

Stretching The Budget

A magnificent effect can be achieved by spending the greater part of your budget on some beautiful, professional paving work near the house where it will be most often seen, and completing the rest of the walkways in minimum-cost concrete.

Save on expensive rock-work and vary an over-flat area beside your path by piling cement on rubble, moulding it to an acceptable outline and, when dry, painting the whole mass a gleaming white. A useful tip from one of the Costa del Sol's most prestigious garden architects.

A Choice of Plants To Grow Between Crazy Paving Stones

Not every gardener wishes to have paths with plants and flowers growing between the crevices of the stonework. On the other hand, others treat their walkways "like horizontal rock gardens," as one garden designer put it.

The choice is yours. If you would like plants peeping up here and there, try anything that takes your fancy. A mistake is easy to put right by grubbing up the offender at the end of the season.

Here is a list of plants which do well in various conditions when planted in crevices between crazy paving. A hard-working dozen, some of them will be sure to thrive in your garden.

Alyssum: Grows well in sun or partial shade. Usually white, its flowers can also be lilac, rose or violet. Sow seeds in spring where they are needed to flower, or insert young plants into pockets of soil.

Baby's Tears: Creeping perennial from Corsica and Sardinia with tiny round leaves. Does best in shade or in a partially sunny position. Somewhat tender, it easily regrows after damage.

Bugle: Quickly forms a thick mat of leaves, producing blue flowers on 10-15 cm. spikes. Many varieties have foliage ranging from green to bronze and deep red. Likes full sun or part shade.

Cymbelaria: Low creeping perennial which will withstand some foot traffic. Small pink flowers. Prefers shade. Choose varieties native to southern Europe.

Heron's Bill or **Erodium:** Small but resistant member of the geranium family. Will slowly grow into low, dense tufts with pink, mauve or white flowers. Sun or part shade. Sow seeds in sandy soil or divide existing plants in spring.

Lobelia: Pretty blue, annual flowers which will often grow again if cut down after flowering. Prefers shade. Surface-sow seed and keep moist. Prick out in clumps to final situation. Or buy plants in spring.

Livingstone Daisy: An annual succulent with bright green leaves and brilliant, "daisy" flowers in white, pink, orange and red. Will thrive in bright sunshine and poor soil. Sow seed in warm weather. It will soon come into flower.

Corsican Mint: This smallest member of the mint family grows only one centimetre high and soon fills cracks and crevices between paving with its tiny round, green leaves, producing miniature mauve flowers in summer. Will grow in sun or part shade but needs moisture. Grow from divisions planted in spring or autumn. It gives off a delightful, aromatic scent when crushed underfoot.

Pratia: Creeping stems carry shiny, dark green leaves with white or pale blue flowers. Prefers shade and needs good soil and plenty of water. If damaged underfoot it soon regrows.

Portulaca: Summer annual with fleshy, succulent leaves which grows 15 cm. high. The brilliant flowers in red, pink, orange, yellow and white normally open fully only in sun and close when the sun goes. The new strain Cloudbeater does not close its blooms at all in daytime. Sow seed in place where it is to flower in early summer, or use young plants. Drought-tolerant, but even better with some watering. Self-seeds.

Creeping Thyme: Forms a soft, flat mat 5-15 cm. high. Fragrant to step on. Small white to mauve flowers in summer. Prefers full sun or light shade. If it becomes too "leggy", cut back and it will re-sprout. The leaves can be used for seasoning.

Violet: The famous scented violet which gives its name to the colour. Also in white and pink. Green, heart-shaped leaves. Grow in shade and give water. Sow seed or put in plants in late winter. Once established it is self-perpetuating. For even better flowers, feed with complete fertilizer in very early spring before the blooms appear.

Natural stone pathway leads through garden to pool and views beyond.
(Photo by W. C.)

This garden path blends in perfectly with its surroundings. (Photo by J. D. D.)

Hibiscus, a magnificent, long-lived flowering bush. (Photo by J. D. D.)

Long-lasting Hydrangeas are massed with flowers. (Photo by AGE)

The Brilliant
Bushes of Spain

LOWERING shrubs are one of the riches of a Spanish garden.
Once planted, they flourish for years with very little attention,
and fill the garden with an almost year-round parade of colour
and scent.

Other shrubs are grown largely for their foliage or interesting and ar-
resting shapes. For the most part they will also be with you for the lifetime of the garden.

How to Plant
Dig a hole that is wide enough to take the full spread of the roots without bending or twisting. Make it deep enough to set the plant at the same
level as it was in the nursery, with 15 cm. of cultivated earth below.

Unless your soil is particularly rich, spread a little well-rotted manure or compost in the bottom and then cover it with a layer of soil so that the roots of the new shrub will not come into direct contact with the manure.

If you buy a container-grown bush, knock it out of its pot and see if it is root-bound, that is, with many roots showing circling round. In this case gently tease some roots free before planting, leaving the main body of the soil-ball intact. Do this, and your ornamental shrub will establish itself more quickly.

If the plant is not pot-bound, don't touch the root-ball. Make the hole 10 cm. wider than the pot all round, so that there will be cultivated earth for the roots to expand into.

When planting any shrub, fill in with loose soil, treading it gently but firmly to see that there are no pockets of air. Then water well.

After-Care

Keep a special eye on the new arrival until it has settled down and started to grow. You will see when more water is needed or if the wind has rocked the plant loose and it needs re-firming. Minor events dealt with promptly mean that there is no check to the plant's development.

As shrubs give so much pleasure for so little work, choose those which naturally like the conditions prevailing in your garden.

If you are new to a district, look round to see what does well in neighbouring gardens. Easy shrubs are as beautiful as difficult ones, and exciting experiments can come later.

As to siting: plant shrubs in borders, on banks, or to fill odd corners. One of the simplest and very attractive ways is to plant a brightly-flowering shrub in a stretch of green lawn. Cut out the turf in a circle about one metre in diameter and set the plant in the centre. Choose a shrub which will eventually grow upwards and outwards and be covered with a profusion of flowers. Oleander and hibiscus are excellent.

A Choice of Shrubs

Oleander

The oleander grows wild in Spain and looks even better if several different colours are planted not too far apart. White, coral, sugar-pink, blood-red, salmon and lemon are widely available, and look magnificent in high summer, flowering together. Bear in mind when planting that after several years some bushes may grow six metres high and four metres wide, so give enough living room.

If you wish to keep the bush small, shorten the stems after flowering.

The oleander can also be trained into a standard tree tall enough to walk under. Restrict the stems of the young plant to one only, until it has reached the height you want. Then pinch off the leading shoot to encourage the stem to break out into a bouquet of leaf and colour. While the main stem is slender, stake it firmly. Eventually it will thicken and need no support.

Oleanders grow easily from cuttings, which take at almost any time of year. Avoid only high summer and any spells of really bad, winter weather.

You can plant cuttings round the edge of a pot of light soil, but the easiest method is to use a beer bottle. The dark colour protects the emerging roots from light and allows you to judge their development.

Take a firm, young shoot 20 cm. long and remove the lower leaves. Place it in a beer bottle half-full of water, and stand it in a shady place, such as a garden shed.

The crown of leaves above the neck will suspend the stem in the water. In about a month you will have a ball of vigorous roots. Break the bottle and plant your new oleander. It is better to plant it first in a 10-cm. pot, and when growing strongly, plant it out in the open ground.

Hibiscus

The hibiscus, though coming from eastern Asia, China, south-eastern USA and Hawaii (where it blooms all the year round and is the State flower), has taken to the subtropical regions of Spain as though they were its natural home.

Dazzling flowers of this tropical bush fill gardens throughout the summer and late into the autumn, the flowering season depending on the climate prevailing in your garden. If you live in hills where occasional frosts occur, plant hibiscus in the shelter of a south-facing wall and away from the path of winds. The shrub will grow, if not pruned, up to five metres, according to the variety. Recently, smaller shrubs growing to no more than one and a half metres high have arrived on the market, which are very useful for small gardens.

Hibiscus flowers are often 10-15 cm. in diameter and are of two kinds: the well-known single type with five petals, or the doubles with many petals. The edges of the petals may be smooth, wavy or ruffled.

They come in many colours. Perhaps the best known is the archetypal, clear blood red, but you can choose white, pink, yellow, salmon or orange.

The flowers are ephemeral, lasting for only one day when cut, whether in water or out of it. For a flower decoration float them in a shallow dish of water, or arrange them on a plate or in a wide, shallow basket.

How to Care for Hibiscus: Prepare a site with well-draining soil mixed with compost. If you aren't sure whether your soil drains well enough, try this experiment. Dig a hole 45 cm. across and equally deep, and fill it with water. If the water hasn't disappeared in about an hour, find another site for your hibiscus, or use a raised bed or plant it in a container.

Spring and autumn are good planting times, although container-grown plants have a wider planting season. Almost any time will do, except for extremes of weather.

When planting, handle the bush carefully. See that you don't disturb the rather delicate root-ball. Give it plenty of water during hot weather, but reduce water as the temperature begins to fall in autumn.

For extra special hibiscus blooms, give a treatment of a fertilizer containing nitrogen once a month during the flowering season. (To choose a commercial fertilizer, read the label. Nitrogen — *nitrógeno* — is listed first in the constituent chemicals mentioned.) Give the last treatment in September to harden off the plant for the cooler weather.

Pruning: It is important to prune the bushes in January, otherwise they become "leggy" with a few blooms only at the end of the branches, as the flowers appear on new growth. While you are shortening stems, cut out any crossing or overcrowded branches.

Pinch out the end of the stems in spring and summer and you will get more flowers.

Normal pruning will keep shrubs in shape for many years, but if a bush has been neglected, prune away up to one-third of the growth. Shape hibiscus bushes well, and they will bloom most attractively all over the plant.

Take time to dead-head your bushes, and you will be rewarded with an even more dazzling display of brilliant flowers.

The Colour-Changing Hibiscus

For fun and for flower decoration, plant a bush of the colour-changing hibiscus, *Hibiscus mutabilis,* known in the USA as the Confederate rose. (There does not seem to be a popular Spanish name but, given the Latin name, good *vivero* owners know it well).

This member of the hibiscus family has the peculiarity of bearing flowers which change colour as they mature. Opening white, the blossoms become pale pink and later a full, rosy red. Usually a bush carries flowers of the three different shades at the same time.

When Queen Elizabeth visited Nigeria, one dinner-table decoration was made famous by these flowers.

Picked at dawn when white, they spent the day under refrigeration and were still pure white when the banquet began. As the courses came and went, the flowers flushed pink in the hot night and then deepened to rose — a dramatic accompaniment to a royal occasion.

Datura — Angel's Trumpet

The datura is a shrub of exceptional value, and is breath-takingly beautiful covered with long, pendulous, trumpet-shaped flowers. It scents the summer darkness with a haunting fragrance truly evocative of "Nights in the Gardens of Spain."

All varieties, whether white, yellow or orange-red, single or double, are beautiful to look at, but not all are equally fragrant. Check with your supplier, and plant at least one of the fragrant varieties, such as *Datura suaveolens* (white) or *Datura chlorantha* (yellow). Set it near your door and it will welcome you home by scent alone on hot, still nights.

Plant datura in a sunny, sheltered place out of the wind, and water well during the growing and flowering season. In early spring, cut back the stems to one or two buds.

This shrub will withstand some neglect, but for truly magnificent results apply a weak liquid fertilizer once a fortnight in summer.

To grow as a standard, restrict young plants to a single stem until they are well over a metre high, and then pinch out the growing point to produce a head of branches on a bare stem.

The Angel's Trumpet can be grown in a tub, but all varieties are large in leaf and flower and need space.

They are also said to be poisonous.

Lantana

An undemanding shrub from Brazil lantana, with its year-round green leaves and profusion of red and yellow flower-heads, is also known in Spain as *la bandera* (the flag) on account of its likeness to the Spanish national colours. Some varieties have blue flowers mixed among the yellow. There are many other hybrids, too.

Lantana will grow from one to two metres tall, is unfussy as to soil and withstands clipping. Give it sun, infrequent but deep watering and it will succeed. You can apply a little fertilizer occasionally, but too much water and fertilizer reduces flowering.

Prune well in spring to remove any dead branches and to prevent the shrub from becoming woody, and you will be rewarded with an exceptionally long flowering season.

Jasmine

One of the most fragrant of garden shrubs and the basis of many French perfumes, jasmine reached Europe from Persia in 1550. The name derives from an Arab-Persian word meaning "white flower". Check when buying that you are getting a shrubby variety, then pinch out the growing tips or prune regularly to keep a bushy shape. It will be smothered in scented, white flowers in early summer. Give normal garden soil and some watering. Best results are achieved when the bush has full sunshine for some hours of the day.

Philadelphus — Mock Orange

A beautiful and easy shrub which will grow to a height of about three metres in sun or in half-sun/half-shade. The white "orange blossom" flowers with their vivid yellow stamens appear in May and are keenly fragrant.

Philadelphus flourishes in normal garden soil given a little watering. For maximum success pay attention to pruning.

Every year just after flowering has finished, cut out the oldest wood and any surplus shoots right down to the base. A badly neglected philadelphus will respond well to hard pruning. You may lose some blossoms for a season, but the final result will be magnificent.

Leonotis — Lion's Ear

An attractive, small shrub from South Africa, leonotis grows up to two metres high and produces its tawny-orange flowers in circular whorls spaced out along the bare branches. The blooms continue throughout the summer and well into autumn.

An undemanding shrub, the Lion's Ear loves the sun and is drought-resistant.

Malvaviscus

Malvaviscus — or, to give it its botanical identification, *Malvaviscus conzatii* — is one of the most hard-working flowering shrubs in Spanish gardens.

Growing to two metres tall or a little more, it hangs out closed, scarlet, hibiscus-like flowers, 6 cm. long, in profusion all over the bush. It often flowers on every day of the year and is particularly notable in December and January.

Some years ago the malvaviscus was out of favour with nursery gardeners. They knew and liked the shrub themselves, but many of their customers came from the cold climates of northern Europe and preferred the exotic look of the open-flowered hibiscus.

Now the malvaviscus is on sale again, having proved its worth. Give it well-drained soil, some water and a little feeding. When necessary, to improve or maintain the shape of the bush, thin out overcrowded growth and shorten stems in February.

Two Flowering Shrubs
for The Christmas Season

Sparmannia

Sparmannia or African hemp, grows easily in a position where it gets some shelter from the hottest noonday sun.

Commonly used as a house-plant in northern climates, in Spain it makes a fine bush three to six metres high with attractive apple-green leaves and clusters of white and yellow flowers, which are all the more welcome as they appear in winter and early spring.

Water it well and prune every few years to give the height and shape that you want.

Sparmannia can be propagated from cuttings planted in sandy soil in spring. Take a firm, young shoot of about 30 cm. long right back to the main stem. Don't attempt to plant the tips of branches only. The success rate will be far higher with larger cuttings.

Use an individual pot for each cutting to cause as little root disturbance as possible when the time comes to plant out.

Poinsettia

This member of the *Euphorbia* family comes into flower only when it experiences long nights of about 14 hours, so comes into its own at Christmas time and in January.

The true flowers are small, inconspicuous and yellow. The "petals" are in fact vivid bracts which surround them.

The best known are the blood-red stars which cheer gardens at Christmas, although pink, white and marbled forms occur.

The traditional practice is to cut back the woody stems immediately after flowering, early in the year. If it isn't too much of an eyesore, leave the stems until April before cutting back to 30 cm. from the ground. When treated in this way, the sap has time to flow back down the stems to the heart of the plant and the following year's flowers will blaze with extra intensity.

This is a good bush to plant near the wall of the house where it can't be seen from the windows, so that you don't have to look at the naked stems between February and April.

A Choice of Three
For Shape Rather Than Colour

Cortaderia — Pampas-Grass

In a fair-sized garden which is still small enough to view at a glance, create a feeling of interest and privacy by planting a few clumps of pampas-grass. Their chief value is the dense, round clumps of enduring green "grass". Behind them one can lounge with a book at peace, untroubled by the gaze of passers-by.

At the end of summer they will throw up bold fronds in cream or dusty pink, which are useful for dried flower arrangements.

Cut down the clumps in midwinter (some gardeners burn them) to promote new growth.

Cyperus — Umbrella Plant

Not to be confused with cypress, this water-loving sedge is a member of the *Papyrus* family, used in ancient Egypt as writing material.

Only attempt to grow it where water is plentiful, or where the underlying water-table is high. Plant it in full light and it will reward you with an interesting clump, one to one and a half metres tall, of green, graceful heads like the ribs of an umbrella, carried on three-sided stems.

Cyperus is easy to propagate by separating an off-set from the main clump.

Another and interesting method is to take a young "umbrella" head, trim it to a diameter of 5 cm. and put it upside-down in half a jar of water, in a good light but out of direct sunlight.

Soon, white roots will appear growing downwards, and at the same time shoots will grow upwards. The cutting works in both directions at once.

When a good root cluster has developed, pot up the new cyperus. Keep it moist and in a good light. It grows rapidly and will soon be ready to plant out in the garden.

Agave — Century Plant

The agave came originally from Mexico and is one of the most memorable plants of the Mediterranean. It holds out flat "hands" of yellowish flowers on small branches which spring from a great central pole rising up to six metres in the air.

The plant itself — perhaps it should not strictly be called a bush, but acts as one in decorating the garden — grows as a bold clump of greyish-green fleshy leaves tipped with spines, which curve out from a central core. It grows for several years before flowering, and having flowered, dies, leaving behind much seed and often suckers already growing round the parent plant.

The Swan-Neck agave produces its flowers densely packed on a dramatic curving spike which arches over almost to the ground.

Other Attractive Bushes

So many attractive bushes grow in Spain that one can only mention a few. As with the agave some may not be bushes in the strict sense of the word, but all are long-lasting plants of substance which serve as shrubs to furnish the garden.

Aloe

Over 300 species of aloe grow wild in Africa, Arabia and Madagascar, and all thrive in the same hot, dry conditions as the agave.

Aloes produce "red-hot poker" flowers from late autumn until the blooms are spoiled by winter rains which, according to the year, may be any time from January until March.

Aloe juice is legendary in native medicine as a remedy for burns and inflammation. Tough, resistant plants, aloes will grow almost anywhere provided that the light is good.

Broom

The term "broom" covers look-alike bushes with "pea" flowers which technically go under the name *Cytisus, Genista* and *Spartium.* Several brooms are native to Spain, others come from the Atlas mountains, the slopes of Mount Etna or the islands of the Atlantic.

Plant-breeders have worked on these naturally-occurring varieties so that today you can buy many different ones.

There is the brilliant yellow Spanish gorse. Don't be put off by the name "gorse". Spanish gorse *is* spiny, but in early summer the burst of yellow bloom is amazing.

Delicate white brooms occur, also brooms smothered in pink flowers and others whose flowers are bi-coloured cream and yellow, yellow and crimson or lilac-pink and cream.

How to Keep Your Brooms Happy: Plant with a minimum of root disturbance in a sunny, well-drained position in light soil — a dry bank is excellent. Brooms flower better when the soil is not too good. Given rich feeding they are apt to grow largely and flower scantily — the reverse of what is wanted in the garden.

Pruning: Correct pruning is vital. Never cut into the old wood of a broom. Prune as soon as flowering is over. Remove about two-thirds of the previous year's growth.

Callistemon — Bottle-Brush

An eye-catching, tall shrub or small tree from Australia bearing summer flowers with rich, crimson stamens which look like bottle-brushes.

They love full sun and will stand up to dry conditions, but are at their very best when planted in a well-drained soil which is kept moist. Never prune except in an emergency. Lemon, white and scarlet varieties are also available.

Ceanothus

Sometimes called wild lilac, most of the ceanothus bushes planted in Spanish gardens have been bred from ancestors found growing on hot, rocky hillsides in California.

Ceanothus blooms may be pink or white, but the blue blossom is the most spectacular, covering the bushes in spring.

Cistus — Rock-Rose

One of the wild shrubs of Spain, the rock-rose grows one or two metres high. It is covered in spring with a mass of open, five-petalled flowers which may be pink, white with chocolate blotches or other vivid colour combinations.

The rock-rose is ideal for covering and stabilizing hot, dry banks. Pruning is not essential, but you can cut out one or two of the older, woody stems occasionally to encourage new shoots.

If you plan to give no water at all once the shrubs are established, plant rock-roses carefully. Check that container-grown plants aren't pot-bound. If they are, cut away roots circling on the surface of the root-ball, then spread out the finer roots so that they can find their way down to lower-level moisture. Watch and water for the first season. After that, rock-roses should be able to fend for themselves.

Fuchsia

This beautiful bush came originally from America and New Zealand, and was named after the 16th-century naturalist, Fuch.

Many different varieties have been bred, but there are two main types: the bushes which grow upright, and the spreading and cascading types which are useful in hanging baskets.

All prefer plenty of water, a sheltered place and some protection from the hottest midday sun. Unless your soil is particularly fertile, dig in well-rotted compost. Also sprinkle on a top dressing of general fertilizer at 70 grams to the square metre.

The best time to plant fuchsias is at the beginning of summer, or as soon as the soil has had time to warm up in your garden. With care, they can be planted at many times of the year, provided they are shielded from hot sun and strong winds, and given plenty of water.

The flowering season is long, and you can have beautiful fuchsias blooming in a sheltered spot in your Spanish garden in January.

To Get Maximum Bloom: Fuchsias flower on young wood, so plenty of branches mean plenty of flowers. To make them branch freely, bloom profusely, and to keep the bush in good shape, pinch out the growing tips — "stopping" the professionals call it — two or three times early in the year. Expect the peak of bloom to come about three months after the last stopping.

In a subtropical climate fuchsias have virtually no rest period, so bushes tend to exhaust themselves after two or three years. "Water well and take plenty of cuttings," one Spanish country gardener said. He grew most successful fuchsias.

Taking Cuttings: Fuchsias root very easily from cuttings. Choose a strong, young shoot with three pairs of leaves below the growing tip. If possible find one without a flower bud. If there is a flower bud, pinch it out and remove any other flower buds which appear afterwards. The cutting can't make flowers and roots at the same time, and strong roots are what you need.

With a razor blade remove the lowest pair of leaves and cut through the stem just below the leaf node (where the third pair of leaves used to grow).

Plant the cuttings in pots filled with a half-and-half mixture of peat-based compost and coarse sand. You can substitute perlite for the coarse sand.

To water, stand the pots in a tray of water and then allow to drain. Keep the cuttings out of wind and sun and they will root in two to four weeks.

As soon as they are growing, pot up the cuttings into 7.5-cm. pots. As they get bigger, pinch out the growing tips to leave three pairs of leaves.

When roots fill the pot, change to a pot 2.5 cm. larger, and when the new fuchsia is well established, plant it out in the garden.

To Train a Standard: Standard fuchsias look extremely elegant, particularly if you choose an eye-catching colour such as white.

To make a standard, grow a cutting in the usual way but don't pinch out the growing tip. In this case remove the side-shoots as they appear. Tie in the stem to a cane every few centimetres to keep it straight. At first it will be very slim.

When the stem is as long as you want it, 60-75 cm. is popular, allow three more pairs of leaves to grow, but don't remove their side-shoots. Then pinch out the growing tip.

Now treat the head of the standard as if it were a normal fuchsia bush, stopping the side-shoots as required. It is easier to train a standard in a pot. Move the pot round a quarter turn each week to keep a straight stem and a well-balanced head.

Hydrangea

The hydrangea is a deciduous shrub with many woody stems; shiny, green leaves and large, round flower-heads of pink, red, blue or white. In Spain it grows out of doors all the year round.

In low-lying, hot gardens, plant it in shade. Up in the hills where the air is cooler, it flourishes in full sun, producing so many flower-heads that the shrub looks like a coloured cauliflower with hardly a leaf showing.

It grows one to two metres high in a round, bushy shape. Dwarf hybrids reach about one metre.

Grow in rich, well-drained soil and water freely in spring and summer, moderately in autumn.

Prune after flowering by cutting back stems that have flowered as far as side-shoots or strong buds. The flowers keep their shape for a long time, fading gradually to a pale colour.

Most hydrangeas are pink, and look particularly good mixed with an occasional crimson bush.

Pink hydrangea flowers can be changed to sky blue by burying small pieces of scrap iron, such as old nails, among their roots, or you can buy a "blueing" powder. White hydrangeas can't be induced to change colour.

Hydrangeas make good pot-plants. Choose a substantial container and pay particular attention to watering. Give a liquid feed once a month during the flowering season.

Iochroma

All iochromas come from tropical South America and may have blue, yellow or pinkish-red flowers. Buy when in bloom to get the colour you want. The deep, darker-than-gentian blue sort is perhaps the most dramatic, as it supplies a colour very seldom seen in the garden. The great splashes of long, tube-like dropping flowers come at the end of summer.

A tall, quick-growing shrub, iochroma can grow to three metres. Another method of display is to trail it against a wall. Find it a sheltered position in full sun and give plenty of water. Prune the shrub hard after flowering.

Spiraea

Many types of spiraea are grown in Spanish gardens, mostly with creamy-white flowers.

Often thought of as deciduous shrubs, not all lose their leaves in winter in warm places, nor do they all remain as low-growing bushes.

With the passing years a spiraea can become a multi-trunked tree eight metres high, with a fine, rounded head covered with a foam of flowers in summer.

Pruning: Prune according to the shape of the plant and the time of blooming. Prune spring-flowering types when they have finished blooming (you can jump the gun by cutting the sprays for flower arrangements. They last well in water). Prune summer-flowering varieties in late winter or early spring.

An easy shrub to grow, spiraea prefers a partially shaded site and some water in summer.

Tamarisk

The tamarisk with its airy, pink flowering branches and slender stems loves salty soil, dry conditions, and stands up to winds from the sea. Occurring naturally in Spain, it may grow from three to 10 metres tall and looks its best in an informal part of the garden.

Plant tamarisks in autumn or at the end of winter. If you wish, prune early-flowering types immediately after blooming, shortening stems to keep the shrubs tidy and cutting out exhausted branches. Prune summer-into-autumn-flowering types in early spring, cutting back last year's growth close to the main branches. This improves the quality of the flowers.

Tamarisks are easy to grow. Take a cutting of a shoot about as thick as your little finger, plant it where it is to remain and keep it well watered.

Yesterday-Today-and-Tomorrow

A type of Brunfelsia *(Brunfelsia pauciflora "Floribunda"* to be exact). Yesterday-Today-and-Tomorrow gains its name from the three shades of flowers it carries on the bush at the same time: "yesterday" purple, "today" lavender, "tomorrow" white.

It is a spectacular bush covered with an immense wealth of blossom, with a long season, as flowers come in waves in spring, summer and autumn. Plant it where you can get full advantage of the spectacle.

Give it good, well-drained soil in a sheltered place with plenty of water. If necessary, prune in spring to keep the bush in shape.

A truly spectacular shrub well worth seeking out.

Flowers
in a Spanish Garden

 new house needs a new garden; or if you take over an existing garden it may not contain all those flowers you wish to see during the changing seasons of the year.

Geraniums

One of the most popular and successful flowers in Spain. They are known to specialists as perlargoniums, who reserve the name geranium for what is popularly known as the Cranesbill. But for most of us they remain geraniums. "It's hard to be botanically correct and conversationally clear," as one American expert remarked. "Gardeners use the word geraniums to speak of the whole works."

If gardeners use the word pelargonium at all, it is to describe the big, stately Lady Washington geraniums, sometimes called regal geraniums, with their large, dramatic flowers.

There has been so much development — much of it recent — since geraniums reached Europe from South Africa more than 250 years ago, that a new world of shapes and colours is now available. Perhaps the most important innovation is the introduction of geraniums that can be raised from seed, which open up a wide choice to gardeners. The climate of Spain brings outstanding results easily — results which often take much attention and expense to achieve elsewhere.

It is easy to buy plants and quickly enjoy the results. But tastes and needs vary, so it is worth exploring the full range of geraniums to see that you are getting the best of what you need and fancy.

You may need bedding plants in mass or singly, pot-plants for terrace or patio, ivy-leaved trailers to cover a bank, hang from a basket or to use as climbers. You might enjoy coaxing a standard to rise on a bare leg and break out into a bouquet of bloom at the head.

Variegated and Coloured Leaves — Some enthusiasts collect rare geraniums with variegated and coloured leaves — rather more expensive than the common run — such as Violet Lambton, which has bronze, yellow and green leaves and violet flowers. You can own a geranium with silver leaves and bright red flowers, or the unusual variety named Freak of Nature, which has pure white stems, white butterfly markings on green leaves and scarlet flowers.

Miniature Geraniums — For some people, small is beautiful. Miniature geraniums grow about 20 cm. high, make good pot-plants, useful front-of-border plants and are excellent in window-boxes smothered in flowers. About a hundred varieties are in circulation, although as with other fancies, you have to build up a collection item by item as and where you find them. Seeds of one variety, the Video series, are now being offered by Thompson and Morgan, Ipswich, England, in mixed colours. Being F_1 (first filial) hybrids — that is, hand pollinated from pedigree parent stock — outstanding performance is to be expected. They grow 20-25 cm. high with multi-headed flowering and zoned, bronze foliage. Grow in a light place protected from wind and heavy rain.

Popular Geraniums

Collectors apart, most gardeners concentrate on one or more of the most popular types of geranium.

Geraniums, flowers from South Africa that have made their home in Spain.
(Photo by J. D. D.)

Four classic flowers from a Spanish garden (clockwise from left); Carnations, Lantana, Roses, and Sunflower. (Photo by AGE)

Common geraniums are sometimes called zonal geraniums because of the dark band usually present on the leaves. A magnificent pot-plant for terrace or patio, you can have flowers all the year round in pink, scarlet, salmon, red-and-white or pure white. Breeders have even produced speckled blooms and geraniums with flowers of different colours growing on the same head.

A bedding variety which doesn't take too much looking after is Disco Dancer (obtainable as seed) which was specially bred to grow well with less attention than many others. The flowers of these vigorous plants come early, about 15-17 weeks after sowing, and stand a little over 35 cm. tall.

Ivy-Leaved Geraniums are named for their thick, shiny, ivy-shaped leaves. These trailing varieties formerly produced mainly pink blooms. Today the flowers can be mauve, red, white, almost black with a white underside, or white edged and striped with red.

The leaves can be nearly as interesting. Some have silver foliage, others cream and green variegated leaves, or green leaves cobwebbed with cream.

For ground cover, set plants or cuttings close together and peg out the trailing growth in all directions. Stop the leading shoots frequently for a carpet of leaves smothered in flowers.

Star Geraniums — so-called as each separate floweret takes the form of a star — can sometimes be bought as plants and grow well from cuttings but, as one of the more recent introductions, are often more easily obtained from seed.

From sowing to flowering takes from 18-20 weeks depending on light and temperature. An early sowing made in December will produce flowers in April or May. Seeds sown later naturally flower later.

Once in bloom and well cared for, flowering is continuous, and you can take cuttings from established plants. In a 15-20 cm. pot a Star geranium will grow into a spectacular plant, and after 18 months will still be compact at 30-40 cm. high, but have a spread of 50 cm. smothered in bloom.

Scented-Leaved Geraniums are a world apart. They stand with delicate, lacy leaves, flowerless for most of the year, but when the leaves are stirred and handled they release their odour. "They are not common, but sell on sight," one nurseryman told me.

The pervasive perfume of spicy lemon, orange, balsam, nutmeg, rose, apple and peppermint, is the result of the evaporation of water from the foliage, leaving behind concentrated oils.

The scent from rose-leaved geraniums is twice as strong as the perfume of roses, and is mixed with flower essence to make the famous Bulgarian "attar of roses".

Geranium Care

Grow geraniums in the sun and air, although in high summer they appreciate shade during the hottest hours of the day. Dead-head regularly for a long flowering period.

Grow all geraniums on the dry side in well drained soil, but for pot-grown plants, keep an eye on watering owing to the limited amount of earth in the pot.

The standard advice is to water when the soil is dry 3 cm. below the surface. For practical purposes, watering every other day works well for container-grown geraniums in hot weather. In the open garden once or twice a week will normally be enough.

Cut down the watering in spring and autumn. Water pot plants once or twice a week in winter when many will still be blooming.

To encourage heavy flowering in planters or the open garden, feed geraniums when in bloom. A good general fertilizer such as the liquid Plantavit, made by Reckitt and Colman in Bilbao, is excellent used every fortnight, but other good products are on sale. Geraniums also respond well to fertilizers primarily made for tomatoes.

If young geraniums are growing spindly, pinch out the tops. They will throw out new shoots further down, which results in fine, bushy plants.

Prune plants in October or April, cutting the old, woody stems down to 5 cm. To have flowers on your patio all year round, prune some in spring and some in October.

To Take Cuttings

Take a shoot from the parent plant any time from spring to October, avoiding only the hottest weather. See that the shoot has two or three nodes (the nobs on the stem from which leaves can shoot). Check that the growing tip is vigorous and without a flower bud. If there is a bud, remove it. The new cutting can't make roots and flowers at the same time, and good, strong roots are what you need.

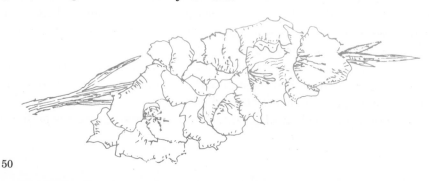

Prepare the cutting by removing all leaves except at the growing tip. Then plant it firmly in well-drained soil with only the bottom node covered.

Cuttings can go directly into boxes, into a container of mixed flowers, or you can plant half a dozen round the edge of a 12-cm. pot. Until the cuttings have rooted, water sparingly and keep them in a good light but out of direct sunlight. Then pot them up singly into 5-cm. pots and pinch out the growing tips.

When the side-shoots are well established, move the new geranium plants into the open ground or into pots one size larger. Don't give too large a pot, as flowering is better when the plants are slightly root-bound.

To Grow from Seed

Specially bred hybrids need a little extra attention while they are getting established. After that they are hardy and trouble-free. From sowing to flowering takes about 18-21 weeks, although some are on record as coming into flower only eight weeks after sowing. Sow from mid-December onwards.

Use a good seed compost such as Levingtons, spacing the seeds out well. Then cover with a thin layer of compost. Water after sowing very delicately, then cover the box with a sheet of glass. Turn the glass daily and remove it after three to five days. See that the compost stays moist but not wet.

For the first few days maintain a steady, warm temperature 21-24 °C is ideal. I have found that a shelf over a hot water tank or radiator proves very successful. Some seeds take longer to germinate than others, anything from three to 21 days.

Transplanting: The seedlings should be transplanted twice. First prick out as soon as the seedlings can be handled, usually about seven to 10 days after sowing.

Make the second move five to six weeks after sowing, potting the young plants up into 7-10 cm. pots. Use a light, free-draining compost and water it gently.

Temperature: After pricking out, try to maintain an air temperature of 21 °C during the day and 18 °C at night — approximately the temperature of a living-room. To encourage rooting, keep at these levels for about 10 days. After that, reduce the warmth gradually until about eight weeks after potting, the night temperature is about 13-15 °C. During the day the temperature can rise to 21-24 °C.

You can grow geraniums at lower temperatures, but they will take longer to mature.

After-Care

Once established, even pedigree geraniums are very little trouble to look after. Give them enough space so that the plants don't touch, and start regular feeding with a liquid fertilizer about four weeks after planting out.

Carnations

These might be called Spain's favourite flower. A carnation held between the teeth of a flamenco dancer; a cascade of blooms from a window-box or a mass of colour and scent in the garden — all are members of the dianthus family, and all, large and small, upright or trailing, grow magnificently in Spain.

You can buy plants, grow from cuttings or sow seeds. You can even grow the large type known as "florist carnations" out of doors. To get the biggest flowers, leave only the final bud on each stem, removing all side-shoots down to the fifth joint. New flowering stems will develop from the lower part of the stalk. Support the plants as they grow tall, unless they are one of the newer varieties with extra-strong stalks, known in Spain as *tallo de hierro,* iron-stalk.

Cuttings

The Spanish method is to take a fine, strong carnation stalk and cut it into lengths of about 10 cm., each containing a node. Plant these, covering the node, round the rim of a pot of sandy soil. Don't over-water. In six or eight weeks when a strong root-system has developed, pot up singly or transfer to the garden.

To Grow from Seed

Sow seed from January to March in a good seed compost, covering lightly. Maintain a temperature of 15-21 °C and expect the seeds to germinate in 14-21 days. Move into a box or individual, small pots when they are large enough to handle and plant in larger pots or out in the garden in April, spacing 25 cm. apart. Keep well dead-headed for continuity of bloom.

All types of dianthus love a good, rich soil.

Stocks

Stocks, often offered in the baskets of street flower-sellers in compellingly attractive form and scent, are not always available as plants just when you need them.

Many new, brilliant and labour-saving varieties are on offer as seed, to grow either as annuals or biennials. Seed packets and catalogues give detailed information.

If you are sowing in later winter or spring for summer flowers, aim for a temperature of about 15 °C, possibly best achieved by choosing a place on a terrace, sheltered from heavy rain. The seeds will germinate in 10-14 days. Move the seedlings into the open garden when danger from storms is past. Some varieties will give you a mass of bloom by Easter, either in pots or in the open garden. Other varieties (labelled "biennial") are planted in autumn, from September onwards, for early spring flowers.

"Selectable" Varieties

The name given by the horticultural trade to those varieties which save you trouble in telling, by their appearance very early on, which will bear single flowers and which double. You then eliminate the singles and concentrate on the gorgeous double blooms to come.

Suttons and Thompson and Morgan both offer seeds by mail order of stocks with this useful peculiarity, under the names Park and Excelsior. Only the yellow-green, palest seedlings will produce double flowers. For positive identification, sow at 12-16 °C. When the first true pair of leaves has formed, lower the temperature to under 10 °C. This cooler temperature makes it easier to distinguish between the "goodies" and the "baddies".

A new breakthrough makes identification of future double blooms of one other variety even easier to spot at an early stage. "Dwarf Stockpot Mixed" is an exceptionally dwarf, hyacinth-flowered stock. The future double-flowering plants show a distinctive notch in the first true pair of leaves. Discard the unnotched plantlets. The carmine-red, rose, purple or white flowers will be with you in two months, 20-25 cm. high, fully double and beautifully fragrant.

Perennials

Old friends such as roses, lavender, pinks and marguerites bloom in Spain as never before in the countries where most of us have lived. Delphiniums and London Pride, Michaelmas daisies and verbena crowd the gardens. Much is familiar but there are new friends to meet, with a lasting and exotic beauty which belies their ease of cultivation.

Pride of Madeira — Echium
This stands up to poor soil and coastal conditions provided the drainage is good. The plant grows with the years to form clumps which throw up great, blue flower spikes. It will survive a considerable amount of neglect, but flowers increase if the dead heads are removed.

The Bird-of-Paradise Flower — Strelitzia
This is familiar in florists' shops in cold climates for its exotic orange or blue flowers, which look rather as if a bird of paradise has landed on the stiff flowering stem. The plant blooms intermittently throughout the year, with rather more flowers in spring and autumn. Feed it well, but divide the clumps infrequently, as strelitzias bloom better when crowded. Plant in a place where there is shade for a short time during the hottest hours. It grows well in planters, and is the official flower of the city of Los Angeles.

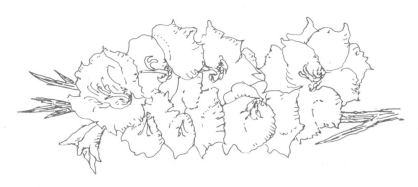

The Ice-Plant

Don't be misled by the name which covers several varieties of tough succulents, all low-growing. Buy plants in bloom, or take cuttings from a plant you know, to get the particular shade of large, brilliant flowers you prefer. All will withstand drought once they are established, but do better with a little water. Feed lightly in autumn.

Gazania

Very many variations of this daisy-type flower give a dazzling display of blooms up to 10 cm. wide, borne on stems 20 cm. tall. The trailing variety looks particularly good when allowed to cascade over a wall. All will grow in almost any soil. Water occasionally, every week or fortnight according to conditions, and give a fertilizer in spring.

Four o'Clock

This perennial gets its name from the fact that flowers open in mid-afternoon. The tall, many-branched stems grow quickly to give the plant almost the look of a shrub, with trumpet flowers of red, white and yellow variations. Sow seed in early spring in an open position for flowers from July into autumn. It will frequently re-seed itself.

Sunflower

The sunflower and all the daisy family thrive in Spanish gardens, including the Shasta daisy, the daisy bush, the Swan River daisy and Felicia; the last two both being a very attractive blue. Plant your garden with a framework of perennials. They will bloom for you every season.

Biennials

The dividing line between biennial plants — which are sown one season for flowering the next — and annuals, which complete their life cycle in one year, becomes a little confused in Spain, as some plants grow and flower more quickly and last longer than one might expect. Others sown in autumn will survive the winter and flower early in the spring.

Hollyhock

Formerly thought of as a biennial, the hollyhock may grow, flower and seed in one year. At least one variety is perennial, while others, performing in their biennial capacity, produce so many seedlings that one is never without flowers during their summer season, year after year.

Older varieties are tall; modern strains shorter. Both bear the familiar hollyhock blooms and perform excellently.

Sweet William
Normally seeds are sown in spring for flowers the following year. Specially selected strains (consult your seedsman or the instructions on the seed packet) bloom in summer from an early spring sowing.

Honesty — Lunaria
This is an example of a true biennial which normally behaves like one. Sow seed in autumn or spring. It is not fussy about soil. The silvery pods are useful for dried flower arrangements.

Annuals

A host of annual flowers grow well in Spain. Take into account the fact that spring comes very early, and sow seeds of hardy flowers like nasturtiums in autumn. The little Tom Thumb variety is excellent for pots and borders. The larger, rambling kind will cover an unsightly corner.

Antirrhinum
Sow seeds in autumn or spring, or buy plants from a nursery. Will grow as a perennial, but the straggling growth and flowers are not worth the space they take up. Renew each year.

Larkspur
The annual delphinium. Sow seeds in autumn or spring where they are to flower.

Clarkia
Clarkia is a name which often includes godetia, a wonderful choice for sunny Spanish gardens. Sow the seeds in autumn where you want them to flower. They grow in the cool season and bloom in spring and early summer. Use them in mixed borders or in sweeping masses of colour. Cut sprays keep for several days if picked when the top bud opens. The other buds open successively. Clarkia grows best in a sunny place in sandy soil, without added fertilizer.

Salvia
Salvia comes in many kinds, but the scarlet annual variety is one which brightens up the garden. The seeds take time to mature. Why not take

a short cut and buy young plants from the nursery?

Shirley Poppy
Sometimes known as the Flanders poppy. Broadcast the seed mixed with sand at intervals during spring and summer to prolong the flowering period. If you have a stone wall, try to introduce a few seeds into the crevices. If you succeed, the result is breath-taking.

Sweet Pea
Plant seeds between October and early January in deeply dug, rich soil. Provide good supports. When the flowers come, strip the plants daily to encourage fresh bloom. Heat-resistant varieties include Cuthbertson's Floribunda, and Knee-Hi, the dwarf strain developed in California by Thompson and Morgan. These need no support. Normal garden watering.

Cut-and-Come-Again Annuals
Lobelia, petunia and phlox will usually flower again another year if the plants are cut down at the end of summer, and the roots kept gently moist during the winter.

Lobelia prefers good soil with plenty of water and shade; petunias need light, reasonable water and good soil. Plant the seeds of phlox in autumn, in rich soil and in good light.

Many other annuals grow extremely well in the Spanish climate, producing lovely flowers for little trouble and cost. Just sow them thinly where you want them to grow. They include: ageratum, amaranthus, English marigold, candytuft, clarkia, Californian poppy, annual sunflower, now with dark red flowers as well; busy Lizzie, African marigold, French marigold, tobacco plant, love-in-a-mist, pansy. Will re-seed freely in the garden. Many most attractive, long-blooming strains have recently been introduced. Petunia, portulaca, rudbeckia, salvia, scabious, verbena, zinnia.

Roses

THE rose is the most famous and valued flower in the world and has been grown in Spain for at least 800 years. An old Arab manuscript gives detailed and sophisticated instructions for developing roses to the full. Arab gardeners could change the colour of the blooms (saffron inserted under the bark produced yellow roses; indigo, blue).

Flowering time was prolonged by covering budded sprays with clay pots, or by firing bushes at the end of summer to encourage new growth.

Today we have an infinite variety of these beautiful flowers, and thanks to the dedicated work of the rose-breeders they bloom nearly all the year round.

So many variations have been evolved that there is a rose for every situation in the garden. You may buy locally or import from abroad, singly or in quantity.

Roses fall into four main types: hybrid teas, floribundas, climbers (those tall-growing roses which today include the types formerly known as ramblers) and miniatures.

Hybrid Teas

These acquired their name when the roses which the Victorians in England thought smelt of China Tea were crossed with repeat-flowering varieties, to emerge as beautifully-shaped blooms growing on bushes about a metre high.

For some years emphasis was placed on the colour and shape of the flower. Now fragrance is back in fashion.

The large and shapely blooms which grow on these bushes are often produced one on each stem. When more buds appear, some gardeners prefer to remove them to produce a flower of maximum effect.

Other modern varieties give roses in elegantly-spaced clusters. The height of these bushes ranges between one and one and a half metres, with some varieties reaching rather more.

Take full advantage of this height differential when planning your plantings. Mound up the soil in the middle of an island bed with tall roses forming a high, central point, graduating down to small bushes at the perimeter. Catalogues are explicit as to height, and nursery gardeners knowledgeable and helpful. Plant hybrid tea rose bushes 45-60 cm. apart.

Standards are rose bushes which have been grown on a single "leg". The growers graft a "bud" on each stem at about one metre from the ground, which then grows out into a well-balanced and shapely head.

Try some beside a path and they will present roses at eye and nose level. They are also exceptionally easy to look after as no stooping is involved.

Floribunda

Floribunda or cluster-flowered bushes, depend for their effect on their massed blooms, and look particularly effective when planted in groups of the same colour. Modern floribundas have taken on the same, elegantly-shaped flowers as the hybrid teas, which accounts for their growing popularity.

A happy fancy is to buy different styles of the same rose. You may have to choose a popular variety to find the right stock available, but the salmon-pink Elizabeth of Glamis, for instance, can often be had. It makes an eye-catching, round bed with a standard rose in the centre surrounded by floribundas of the same colour.

These roses also make excellent hedges about one metre high. Floribundas are usually planted 35-45 cm. apart, but those which make a spreading bush up to 120 cm. tall need 45-60 cm. of living room between them.

Climbing Roses

These are the stiffer-stemmed type of tall-growing roses, with flowers like hybrid teas or the modern floribundas. They are particularly suitable as permanent features growing up the wall of a house.

Choose a colour that will look its best against your wall. Brilliant red looks spectacular against a white wall, while pink or copper coloured set off stone or brick.

Ramblers, like climbers, are tall-growing roses which need support and produce masses of blooms in summer. They have more pliant stems and so are ideal for trellises, pergolas and archways.

A few roses grow so vigorously and to such height that the specialists have dubbed them "rampant", meaning that they will grow over and up almost anything. Such a rose is Rambling Rector, with semi-double, creamy-white flowers produced in big clusters. Use this one for a huge display. It will ramble out sideways and grow upwards to six metres or more, and apart from any essential restraint needs no pruning. Indeed, it has been called "impenetrable and unprunable."

Plant both climbers and ramblers two metres apart and see that their supports are sound.

Another attractive use for a single climbing or rambling rose, is to train it up a pillar, forming a column of colour.

Dense, low-growing roses with plenty of leaves make attractive ground cover. Hoe the ground in April or May and they will suppress most weeds for the rest of the year.

The 150 cm.-high Scabrosa (nobody knows where this rose came from) will grow into a bush equally wide, bearing big, mauve flowers contrasting with vivid yellow stamens. When the flowers have finished it is still attractive with round, red hips looking like small tomatoes.

If you prefer low ground cover, try the pink Fairy from England, less than a metre high and covering about a square metre of land. This easy, "cushiony" bush produces sprays of perfect little roses ideal for cutting, and when not in flower the small, shining leaves are still attractive.

Miniature or Patio Roses

These smaller delights are particularly useful to grow in small beds in patios or town gardens, or in pots where the garden soil is particularly bad. In a planter you can see that soil conditions are perfect.

Recently, a few of these mini-roses have come on to the market in standard form. There are now not only small roses growing on short, standard stems, but some, like the miniature standard Snow Carpet, will even trail downwards, giving the effect of an overflowing cascade of white.

Although small roses are useful for small spaces, you can grow almost any variety of rose in a sizeable container, such as a half-tub or large pot.

How to Care for Your Roses

Roses need a well-drained fertile soil, water and plenty of light. Keep them out of the wind and if necessary provide a wind-break. Bright, well-formed roses grow in a sheltered, peaceful atmosphere.

Either buy roses bare-rooted or already planted in a container. Experts prefer to buy bare-rooted bushes so that they can see what they are getting, both above and below. Other gardeners welcome the container plants offered by the *viveros*.

Bare-rooted bushes are only available during the dormant season. Never buy once they show signs of breaking into bud. For best results, plant by the end of February. Container-grown roses can be planted at any time of year except for high summer or spells of really bad weather.

Planting

Prepare a rose-bed by digging it over thoroughly and enriching the soil with well-rotted manure and compost, although the roots of the bushes must never come into direct contact with manure. The soil should be well-drained but not dry.

Dig a comparatively shallow hole for the rose bush: 15-17 cm. deep will normally be enough. Dip a bare-rooted bush in water then spread the roots out horizontally in the hole. Fill in rich soil around the roots, treading it and making certain that the bush is firm, and that even if the soil dries out a little there will be no air pockets. Note the mark showing the previous soil level and plant to the same depth.

Next, cut the stems down to 10-15 cm. from ground level. The rule in pruning roses is that the weaker the growth the harder you cut.

For a standard rose, drive in the supporting stake before planting. Put it well down below root level and tie in the stem carefully.

When planting roses bought in containers, dig the hole, remove the container carefully so as not to disturb the root-ball, tread the bush firmly into place, give it a bucket of water and tread again a few days later.

Growing Roses in Pots

Roses need slightly different preparation for containers than when planned for the open ground. First, prune the roots so that all will fit into the pot without bending or twisting.

After filling the pot half-way, build and then firm a cone of soil to fit under the pruned root system.

Spread the roots out over the cone and check the final height of the plant in the pot (set it so that the bud union — the swelling where the rose was budded on to its root-stock — is level with the pot rim). Add more soil, firming it as you go, until the pot is filled to about 3 cm. from the rim.

Finally, water until the pot drains, then water again. Add more soil if necessary. Repot every two or three years, or less frequently if the rose continues to thrive.

Pruning

January is an excellent time to prune roses in Spain. Prune existing rose bushes by cutting out all very old, weak, crossed or damaged stems. Then shorten the remaining stems to an outward-facing eye, on a stem that is about as thick as a pencil. When in doubt, over-prune rather than under-prune roses.

When pruning standard roses, don't prune away more than half the total volume of the head.

For climbing roses, cut out weak or damaged growth and only prune other stems to fit into the space available.

Rambler roses perform best when pruned thoroughly each autumn. Detach all growth from the support. Spread it out on the ground and cut out the stems that have flowered. Then choose the best of the new shoots (about three shoots per plant) and tie them back into place. Rambler roses flower only on small side-shoots growing on second-year wood.

After-Care

After pruning, top-dress your roses with compost and manure or use a compound fertilizer. Give plentiful watering continuing throughout the season.

In March, as the buds are forming, give another application of fertilizer, and again two months later to help the plant through the summer.

Some rose growers spray regularly each fortnight, against such troubles as rust and black spot, with one of the many good products available. Rose pests can also be dealt with by spraying with an insecticide such as Hexyl. But if you wish for a garden full of birds and butterflies, avoid chemicals as far as possible. A solution of pure soap and water can be used to remove greenfly, and strong, healthy roses rarely attract many parasites.

Dead-head roses regularly to encourage fresh blooms. Plant new roses in a place where roses have not grown before, or dig out the old soil to a depth of 50 cm. and replace with fresh earth.

Roses bloom from spring to Christmas time in Spain. (Photo by J. D. D.)

Lush vegetation keeps a Spanish patio cool in summer. (Photo by W. C.)

Patios, Balconies
and Window-Boxes

ATIO gardening is the art of gardening in bright colours, often contrasted with white walls and black ironwork. It is a legacy of the Roman occupation of Spain, later taken over by the Arabs who transformed the austere, classical patio into a haven of peace and pleasure filled with sunshine and shade, the scent and colour of flowers, singing birds and the splash of fountains.

Balconies and window-boxes also adorn a home. Even in large gardens, focal points — close to the house for instance or beside a seat — can be enhanced by vivid container plantings, which can be renewed with the changing seasons. Also, by the use of pots and tubs filled with special soil, you can grow plants which would not tolerate the normal soil in your garden.

Planning and caring for a patio or balcony is one of the most reward-ing forms of gardening. Each will be an extension of the home; an extra room with the feeling of being both indoors and out at the same time. And they need not entail too much maintenance if the plants are carefully chosen.

First of all consider containers. In a patio there may be some beds open to the earth beneath, but you will need extra planters for added variety. Amost anything will do. I have seen plants grown successfully in oil drums, a teapot, even large sea-shells. (Choose a strong plant like a geranium for an experiment like this. The result can often be a bonsai-like miniaturization).

But most of us prefer containers of a more conventional type. Tradi-tional flowerpots with their warm look go well with any type of plant. Plastic pots need less watering as evaporation cannot take place through the sides. Also there are outsize Ali Baba jars for really big subjects.

The *cerámica* offers choices both utilitarian and interesting, from big, oblong, concrete "flower-beds" to planters of reconstituted stone in tra-ditional or modern styles.

Leaving aside for the moment the question of soil, the first rule for suc-cessful container gardening is to use pots with good drainage. Normal flowerpots with a central hole need only a few broken pieces of pot dropped into the bottom before being filled with soil. When shopping for large containers, look out for adequate drainage holes and, if possible, small feet to lift them off the ground.

As for soil, the easiest way of getting the right type is to go to an expe-rienced nursery gardener, explain your needs and buy what he suggests. If you have good earth available in your garden, it may be cheaper to amend this to get a well-balanced potting medium.

The aim is to get a light, friable, easily-drained, nourishing soil which will retain moisture well enough to avoid over-frequent watering. To achieve this, mix heavy soil with sharp river sand, and light soil with rich loam. Add granulated peat to retain moisture, and some good fertilizer to nourish the plants.

As the soil in big containers is unlikely to be changed entirely for some years, it is worth taking the trouble to get a good basic mixture to begin with. Ideally, soil should be changed each year, but with regular feeding and the addition of some new earth to the top of the pot each spring, containers usually remain successful with the same soil for many years.

Hanging Baskets
Added plant space and interesting effects come with the use of hanging

baskets. Remember to site them out of draughts and in a place where you will be able to water them without too much trouble.

The traditional type of hanging basket is made of a framework of galvanized wire. Old-time gardeners used a lining of reversed turfs before adding soil. This had the advantage that trailing plants could actually grow down through the turf, as well as spill out over the edge, producing an attractive effect.

The modern practice is to line the basket with plastic, put a handful of charcoal in the bottom to keep the soil sweet, and then fill up with potting compost.

Hanging baskets are also available in plastic, which is less durable, or in natural materials such as wood or macramé. Line either with foil, or fill with plants in individual pots.

Remember that when planted up, a hanging basket is heavy, so attach its suspension wires to a strong hook.

Use plants of three different types: trailing and "flopping" plants for the edge, which will cascade gently downwards, softening the outline and hiding the underneath of the basket; medium flowers to form the main visual impact, and finally, a tall subject in the centre to give a focal point to the whole arrangement.

Trailing plants: Edge your basket with lobelia, asparagus fern or cascading, pink geraniums.

Medium flowers: Petunias, especially the scented white variety, geraniums, achimenes (the Hot Water plant), fuchsias and begonias.

For the centre of the basket: If you have a central wire, try a climbing flower like Morning Glory or passion flower. If not, the taller of the medium flowers such as fuchsia and geranium, make an attractive mounding effect. Try to have at least three different flowers in harmonious combinations of colour. The possibilities are endless.

Window-Boxes

Treat window-boxes much as hanging baskets. The main differences are that they do not need lining and are much easier to reach for cultivation and watering.

As with hanging baskets, see that they are very firmly secured. Check that the drainage holes are adequate, and fill with good potting soil. After that, you have an extremely wide choice. On the open side concentrate on cascading flowers, with a riot of carnations, petunias and ivy-leaf geraniums cascading downward. If you still have space, try cacti and succulents in a hot place, mini-roses in *sol y sombra* or even a collection of herbs, such as mint, chives, sage and feverfew in a shady window-box near the kitchen.

The Patio

A patio should be arranged to direct the eye to different levels. A wistaria or vine trained overhead will not only give shade from the midday heat, but also a mass of purple flowers in early spring from the wistaria, or welcome grapes in autumn from the vine. A white mandevilla — sometimes known as king jasmine — loads the summer air with scent from its bright, white flowers, growing from ground level high into the air.

Hang up a wall of flowers with geraniums and carnations spilling exuberantly from pots.

Build ledges at different levels. In a corner catching the morning sun, place a wide, shallow dish of violets. The scent will surprise you.

In a lighter position try mixed containers, using flowers of the same shade but different shapes. Salmon geraniums for instance, partnered by salmon busy Lizzies, made more vivid by the contrast of white petunias and cooled by the silver leaves here and there of cineraria maritima, make a combination to be remembered.

Or for impact, try a planter filled with one flower of one colour only, such as a pink-red geranium. Soften the outline of the rim with little trails of ivy.

Dishes of annuals such as dwarf nasturtiums or blue lobelia are cheap and easy to grow.

A single Madonna lily or amaryllis in a pot adds distinction. Or soften a shady corner with a cool collection of ferns.

Patio Trees

Trees make interesting features on the patio. They can also be useful on a balcony or roof garden to cut out noise from neighbours and give a real sense of privacy and country atmosphere in the city.

Arbor vitae or **Thuya:** As one Spanish nurseryman told me, "The thuya is one of the conifers which grows best in Spain." It is tough, does well by the sea, and makes a good container tree. The variety *orientalis* has green foliage and forms a compact pyramid. There is also a golden version.

The variety *enana,* dwarf, is globe-shaped and grows more slowly.

Leave specimen trees unpruned for as long as possible, although badly placed branches can be removed in spring.

To make a protective roof-top hedge, space 60 cm. apart (from the trunk, as pot sizes vary) for trees one metre tall; 75 cm. for trees up to 125 cm., and one metre between each for taller trees. Clip twice in the year, once in late spring and once in midsummer.

Bay: The green bay tree is an ideal plant for use in patio, roof-top or town situations as it grows well in pots, can be clipped into interesting shapes or used to form a dense, evergreen hedge.

To give your home added distinction, flank a doorway with two bay trees grown as standards, their straight, bare stems supporting green globe heads.

Bay-leaves are also useful as herbs in cooking.

The bay tree must have well-drained soil, but it is not a thirsty plant. Give only enough water to prevent the soil drying out.

Cypress: Many members of the cypress family are available in nurseries and make good container plants for patios and roof gardens. The compact Arizona cypress is one of the best, with its close-growing foliage. There are many other varieties with dark green, grey-green, blue-green and golden foliage. All are tough and put up with regional differences in soil and weather conditions. Plant — in spring or autumn — from containers, as the cypress resents root damage.

Papaw: In the shelter of a patio you can grow papaws in areas where cold winds would otherwise kill them. Plant three or four together in pots or in a patio bed, as both male and female papaws are needed to produce fruit. Choose a sunny or lightly shaded position.

The plants may grow six metres tall, or more. If they outstrip the protection of the patio and are caught by cold winter winds, immediately cut off the damaged part to prevent the trouble spreading. Don't attempt to grow as permanent trees. The fruit is grown on young plants. Give plenty of water and fertilizer in warm weather.

Yucca: The yucca is an excellent feature plant for the patio or roof garden. In an emergency it will survive drought, although if you have to be away for long periods it is unlikely to flower.

If possible, choose the small variety, Spanish Dagger, although any yucca bought small will grow more slowly in a pot than in the open garden.

Don't choose any yucca for use in a confined space as the leaves are sharp.

Care for Patio Trees
For all container-grown trees apply a general fertilizer in spring and autumn, and add 10 cm. of good, new soil to each pot in spring. If necessary remove some of the old soil to make room for the new.

Bulbs, Corms and Tubers
For House and Garden

HAT is a bulb? Experts group under the general heading of "bulbous plants" three distinct types — bulbs, corms and tubers. All of them store within themselves food and embryo flowers for the coming year.

A "bulb" has embryo flower buds and leaves growing from a flat disc at the base. These are protected by fleshy layers, as in an onion or a tulip.

A "corm" is a swollen stem base storing food and future flowers in a solid mass. The crocus and gladiolus are familiar examples.

"Tubers" are swollen underground branches with "eyes" from which the new plants grow. Among the best known are potatoes and dahlias.

In practice all "bulbs" share a special advantage. Sensibly chosen, planted and cared for, the result is sure to be a beautiful display of flowers.

Bulbs for Christmas Flowering in the House

Thanks to the expert work of the bulb breeders, there are varieties which can be relied on to come into flower during the 12 days of Christmas.

After being lifted from the fields, the bulbs have been treated in special temperature and humidity-controlled chambers, to develop the full potential of the embryo flower and regulate the time at which it will emerge.

This science has come a long way since the historic occasion when a consignment of lily of the valley crowns was stored beside a load of frozen reindeer meat on a long railway journey across Russia. To the amazement of the consignees, the lilies came into flower much earlier than their usual time, and the craft of controlling blooming time by temperature began.

For Christmas flowering, don't stray away from the varieties the breeders suggest. They know which of their products will come into bloom at the right time. Some will even flower before Christmas.

Amaryllis

The amaryllis — *Amaryllis hippeastrum* is its full name — is a big, beautiful and exotic lily which grows particularly well in Spain.

For Christmas flowering, plant the big bulb at the end of October or early in November. Choose a pot with good drainage which will allow at least 3 cm. all round the bulb. Buy a bag of coarse-textured, free-draining potting compost.

If you prefer to make your own, mix good loam and leaf mould, and add enough silver sand to keep the medium porous. This is vital for the proper development of the roots.

Soak the roots and the lower part of the bulb in tepid water for 24 hours. Then put enough soil in the pot to form a cone. Place the bulb on this cone with the roots spread well out and fill up with the soil mixture leaving about half the bulb exposed.

To get the amaryllis going, it needs bottom heat. Put it on a shelf over your hot water tank or on the mantelpiece. Give only a little tepid water during the first two weeks.

At all times water from the top only, and remember to use tepid water. Never allow the pot to stand in water, or the soil to dry out.

To flower by Christmas day, keep your amaryllis in a warm place day and night, maintaining a temperature of about 20 °C. Good light is not important at this stage. Move the plant into a good light, but out of direct sunlight, as soon as a bud forms. Give rather more water and a minimum temperature of 15 °C. The lily will make surprisingly rapid growth now. The thick stalk, or stalks, can shoot up by as much as 5 cm. in a single day. If necessary, support with a cane. Once the flowers open, move the pot to the coolest place in the room.

When buying amaryllis, you can choose red, apple-blossom pink, salmon, orange or white, or from many hybrids of these colours. Each stem carries at least four, very large flowers.

After-Care: In northern countries it is difficult to get an amaryllis to bloom again a second year without a heated greenhouse. In Spain's subtropical climate it blooms again year after year, given the proper treatment. It may even become the parent of another flowering bulb.

To give every chance for more flowers the following year, remove the stem when the flowers have faded but leave the foliage.

Look after the leaves carefully, as it is through them that the bulb gets the vitality to make future flowers.

Place the pot in a sunny, warm place out of doors, and feed the plant once a week with a liquid plant fertilizer. When the leaves turn yellow, cut off the foliage just above the neck with a sharp knife. You can expect one flowering stem for every four leaves that the plant has grown.

Dry the bulb for 10-12 days at about 22-24 °C. A sun-trap corner out of doors does well, provided it is under cover from rain. Store during the winter in the original pot at 14-16 °C. You can leave it in the same sunny, dry corner in the patio.

In January remove the bulb and repot it in fresh bulb fibre. When not needed for Christmas flowering, amaryllis may be planted any time up to the end of April.

Hyacinth

For Christmas flowering in bowls in the house, buy specially "prepared" bulbs. They have had skilled treatment during their dormant period to produce beautiful flowers in December. The size of the bulb is directly related to the size of the flower which will emerge from it.

Watch the following points: plant in good time — not later than the first week in October for Christmas flowering. Use good bulb fibre. Don't try to hurry the results.

Plant hyacinths on a layer of fibre in the bottom of a bowl so that the tops are just below the rim. They can be close together but mustn't touch each other or the bowl. Then add damp fibre, pressing it firmly round the bulbs until it is 2 cm. below the rim of the bowl.

Hyacinths specially prepared for early flowering need at least eight weeks in complete darkness. See that the temperature does not rise above 10 °C (keep it a little lower, if possible) and that the fibre is moist.

When the flower buds are standing well out of the necks of the bulbs, bring the bowls out of the darkness into a subdued light in a rather warmer place. Cover with newspaper for a few days to lengthen the stems still further. Turn the plants every few days to keep the stems growing evenly.

Finally, when the hyacinths stand straight and scented in full and beautiful bloom, stop watering them. It makes the flowers last longer.

If the flower heads are particularly heavy, support them with individual stakes. Place the stake beside the stem and pierce the point straight into the bulb. This won't harm it. Then tie stem to stake just below the flower head.

Among the best varieties for Christmas growing are the light blue Bismark, Delft Blue (a deeper delphinium blue), Pink Pearl and the pure white, highly scented L'Innocence.

You can also grow hyacinths in water alone. Use a special glass to support the bulb just above the level of the water and put a small piece of charcoal in the bottom to keep it sweet. It isn't necessary to keep the glass in total darkness, a shadowy place will do, but grow as cool as possible.

Roman Hyacinth

The smaller, white, more fragile variety of hyacinth will grow in fibre, pebbles (embedded just above the water-level) or in glasses. Plant Roman hyacinths in September for Christmas flowering.

Narcissus

The easiest type of narcissus to grow in the house is the "bunch flowered" narcissus, such as the famous Paperwhite, which can be put in the light immediately after planting.

These narcissi grow wild in many parts of southern Spain, springing up as soon as the rains come, at any time from October to early spring.

The bulbs bred by specialist growers produce even more beautiful flowers.

It is necessary when growing narcissi to find them a cool and moist place to grow in. For this reason they grow particularly well planted in pebbles and water. Plant as soon as they are available. Aim for as low a temperature as can be found in the house in the early, root-forming stage, and then at the end of November move to an airy room with a temperature of 10-12 °C.

Keep the bulbs well away from fires and radiators. This will give healthy growth and a long flowering time.

You don't have to confine yourself to white narcissi. The scented Grand Soleil d'Or (now being raised in Israel) produces deep yellow blossoms with a gold cup, and the flowers of Cragford have creamy petals set behind a bright orange cup.

Tulip

A few early tulips will come into flower for Christmas provided that they are planted before the middle of September.

They need as cool a place as possible to grow in. Choose the coolest place in the garden, facing north and put them in a "plunge bed."

To make a Plunge Bed: The aim is to keep the bulbs cool while they make strong roots.

Bury the pots up to their rims in the soil, then cover with a thick layer of peat, sand or sifted ashes. Light, sifted garden soil will do. Make the covering 15 cm. deep and keep the covering in place with retaining boards.

If you use bowls without drainage holes, protect them from rain, otherwise they will become waterlogged. Wrap decorative bowls in news paper. The paper when damp will be soft enough for the growing shoots to penetrate.

To Plant Tulips: Peel off the papery, brown skin before potting. This makes for stronger roots. Place in pots or bowls in bulb fibre, anchoring them firmly but allowing the top third of the bulb to stand free of the fibre.

Bring the bowls into the house about December 1st. By this time the shoots should be about 10 cm. long. Keep them in the dark at a temperature of about 18 °C. When the plants have grown 3-5 cm. taller, move them into the light. Give an even temperature of not more than 20 °C (average room temperature), and they will have plenty of time to come into long-lasting flowers.

Three Tulips for Christmas
Brilliant Star Maximus — short-stemmed, bright red tulip.
Christmas Marvel — a large-flowered, carmine tulip.
Marshal Joffre — the yellow version of Brilliant Star.

Bulbs for Patio and Garden

Spain is a wonderful country for growing bulbs on the patio and in the garden. When planting make sure that the soil is pressed firmly round the bulb and that there is no air pocket beneath. Some bulbs flower in spring, some in summer and others in autumn. Many can be left to grow and multiply in the soil for many years.

Agapanthus — the African Lily or Lily of the Nile.
Not truly a bulb, the agapanthus is often thought of as such, as it grows from a very thick root-stock. In Spain it also bears the charming name *flores del amor,* the flowers of love, derived from the Greek name. An excellent container plant on the patio.

An accommodating lily, the agapanthus will grow in full sun or in a more shady place provided it gets three hours of sun a day. It does best in loamy soil but will succeed in much heavier types of earth.

Water throughout the growing season, but once established, it will survive periods of drought, such as during a holiday.

This fine, bold blue lily grows about 50 cm. tall, bearing its flowers in large clusters from summer until the beginning of autumn. Divide every five years or so in March.

Allium
A fine, large and ornamental member of the onion family, all alliums come from the northern hemisphere, from China, Central Asia, southern Europe and various parts of the United States.

According to variety, they grow from 45 cm. to well over one metre tall, bearing small flowers in big, round clusters at the end of bare stems. A very few, of which Chinese Chives are one, grow only up to 30 cm. tall.

Allium flowers range through many shades of pink to red, violet and blue. There are also white varieties. Many are charmingly scented, and are excellent for flower decoration and for use as dried flowers. Don't be afraid of the connection with the onion family — even those that do smell of onion only give off the scent when bruised or cut.

Plant the bulbs in autumn in a sunny place and water while growing.

The clumps will enlarge and need very little attention. An eye-catching bulb for the garden.

Arum — Zantedeschia

This lily grows so easily in Spain that it survives for long periods unattended. For best results plant the rhizomes 15 cm. deep and 30 cm. apart in normal garden soil, either in full sun or part shade. Water well in warm weather. It will even grow in wet places.

To grow in a container, plant one rhizome in each 15-cm. pot. Water sparingly until the leaves appear, then water freely. Feed each week with a diluted liquid fertilizer and reduce watering and feeding when flowers fade. Finally, don't water at all until the new shoots appear.

The clumps will increase, giving many large, white flower bracts curving round a central spike of tightly-packed, golden "true" flowers.

Belladonna Lily

This South African lily blooms in August or September, lifting its pink trumpet-shaped, scented flowers out of the earth with no sign of leaves. Four to 12 flowers top each reddish stem.

It grows in most places and is surprisingly long-lived and resistant to neglect. Water an abandoned — seemingly empty — container of Belladonna lilies at the beginning of August, and they will emerge and flower in a very short time. The flower spikes grow about 75 cm. tall, to be followed by strap-shaped leaves in autumn or winter.

Plant as soon as flowering is over, setting the bulb tops even with the level of the soil. Only lift and divide clumps when the colony is overcrowded.

If you disturb the bulbs at the wrong time they may not bloom the following year, or indeed for several years. Don't discard them. They will flower eventually.

Spanish Bluebell

Like the English bluebell, but stronger and more vigorous, the Spanish bluebell is an excellent choice for Spanish gardens. It grows 50 cm. tall and bears a dozen separate bells. Blue is the favourite colour, but there are pink and white varieties.

Once planted it will establish long-lasting colonies.

Plant in the autumn 7 cm. deep, and water from October onwards if the weather is dry. It is necessary that the bulbs dry out in the summer.

The Spanish bluebell is a good container flower and excellent for cutting.

Canna Lily

This flamboyant lily is an old introduction from Central America and probably reached Europe before Shakespeare had written *Hamlet.*

Many varieties are now available in red, yellow, coral, pink, white and bi-colours. The strong stems grow up to two metres tall and there are dwarf varieties. All have large leaves like the banana.

Plant the tuberous roots in spring in rich but loose soil 12 cm. deep and 25 cm. apart in a sunny place. Water well during the flowering season, and when the flowers are over, cut the stalk down to the ground.

There is no need to disturb the root-stock for several years.

Clivia — Kaffir Lily

This striking member of the amaryllis family grows from tubers and appears in April or a little earlier.

The strong stems grow 30-45 cm. tall and carry clusters of bright orange funnel flowers above strap-shaped, green leaves.

Plant the tubers with the tops just above soil level, in a bright place but out of direct sunlight.

Good in the garden, clivias are superb container plants for the patio. Feed them well but don't disturb for many years. They flower best when crowded.

Colchicum — Meadow Saffron

Often called the autumn crocus, the colchicum is not a true crocus and, coming from the Mediterranean region, thrives better in Spain than the crocus as it does not need such cold winters.

Late in the summer the "crocus" flowers of rose, purplish-pink or white, appear from the bare ground. The leaves come in spring and then die back leaving the site bare.

You must plant the corms during their short dormant period in July and August. Plant in sun or very light shade and leave undisturbed (except for watering) for many years, spacing the corms 7 cm. apart and setting them 7 cm. deep.

When the time comes to thin out the colony, don't divide the clumps until 20-30 days after the last flowers have died.

The colchicum has the peculiarity that it will flower freely if the corm is put on a dry saucer in a light place, and given no further attention. After that, the corm must be planted in the garden.

You can also grow it in a bowl on a layer of pebbles 5 cm. deep. Set the corm upright and fill up with water to just below the base. The next year, plant it out in the garden.

Don't confuse the colchicum or meadow saffron with true saffron. Colchicum isn't edible.

Daffodil, Narcissus, Jonquil

All are members of the narcissus family, and good bulbs well planted will grow and increase for years. They are excellent container bulbs for the patio. When deciding on a site, bear in mind that the flowers will grow facing the sun.

All the daffodil-narcissus-jonquil family last well when cut.

Successful Planting and After-Care: Plant deeply. Fifteen centimetres is right for bigger bulbs; cover smaller bulbs with 12 cm. of soil. This gives the plants the necessary moisture during the growing season.

Place the bulbs 20 cm. apart and you won't have to divide them for about three years. One time I didn't do this, and planted a drift of mixed narcissi by the well-known method of throwing the bulbs and planting them where they fell to get a natural look. I threw with too generous a hand. The colony became overcrowded. The quality of the flowers suffered and the bulbs were packed so closely together that it was impossible to get them out without butchery.

Plant narcissi in full sun or light shade. Later-flowering varieties will last longer in bloom if lightly shaded.

In warm Spanish gardens don't plant narcissi until November, to allow the soil to cool down.

If you get your bulbs earlier, unpack them at once and spread them out. They may go bad if kept in their bag for more than a week.

Water after planting and then watch the weather. In an exceptionally dry winter and spring give additional water. Water while flowering.

Good bulbs deserve good treatment. When flowering is over, give a liquid fertilizer every 10 days until the leaves die down. Never cut off the leaves or tie them into knots until they turn yellow.

A good plan is to plant the daffodil family at the back of a border where the flowers can be seen in spring. As later herbacious plants grow up, the dying foliage is hidden.

Gladiolus

The gladiolus is one of the wild flowers of Spain, and the larger cultivated corms grow well in Spanish gardens, from baby varieties about half a metre high to noble spikes rising 160 cm.

Plant the corms any time from January to March in warm, frost-free areas. In fact there is a wide choice of planting time according to local conditions. Where frosts occur, plant as soon as any danger is past. Whenever planted, expect the flowers 65-100 days later.

Give a rich, well-fertilized soil, but don't allow fertilizer to touch the corms directly. Plant the bulbs four times deeper than their height, except when the soil is heavy when they should be planted a little nearer the surface.

Set big corms at a distance of 15 cm. from each other; smaller corms 10 cm. apart. When the plants have grown five leaves, surround them with a good general fertilizer, but don't let it touch the stems. Water it in well.

Water regularly as the gladioli grow, and watch for pests. If necessary use a pest control.

Stake the large stems individually. The baby gladioli probably won't need it.

For use as cut flowers, take the flower spikes as soon as the lowest buds begin to open. Leave at least four leaves on the stem to feed the new corms growing above the old ones.

When the leaves turn yellow, dig up the plants, cut the tops off just above the corms and dry in a shaded, airy place. About three weeks later, pull off the roots and the shrivelled, old corms (now useless) from the base of the new corms, dust with "diazinon" powder — don't use the aerosol version — and store in a cool, airy place.

Freesia
These beautifully-scented flowers grow freely from corms planted out of doors in Spain and reach a height of 30-40 cm.

Plant the corms 5 cm. deep and 7 cm. apart with the pointed end up. Do this in autumn in a sunny place, with well-drained soil, and they will naturalize and become a spread of colour and scent each March.

Freesias also grow well from seed which should be sown in July or August. They grow remarkably quickly and will often flower the following spring.

After flowering, the plants dry. When the foliage turns yellow you can remove it. The freesias come to life again with the autumn rains. If there is no rain, give water.

They are good in containers on the patio and excellent as cut flowers.

Iris
Irises are one of the wild flowers of the Spanish spring, and take their place with ease in the garden.

Out of the many varieties available, choose the fragrant Spanish iris

Tulip time in Spain. Pansies flourish in the foreground. (Photo by AGE)

White Gladioli contrast with blue Delphiniums at the beginning of summer.
(Photo by J. D. D.)

(also known as Dutch iris) which is an easy-to-manage bulb, growing about 50 cm. tall.

Plant 8-10 cm. deep and 10-12 cm. apart in sun or semi-shade in autumn, and if there is no rain, water during the growing season. You can leave the group undisturbed for years until it gets overcrowded, or lift and divide the clumps every three years. Expect the flowers in March.

They make excellent cut flowers and are good in containers. If you need to move them, wait till the leaves have died before digging; store the bulbs in a cool, airy place and don't keep them out of the soil for more than two months.

Lily

The lily is the aristocrat of bulbs and in the last 50 years breeders have produced large numbers of beautiful hybrids, many perfumed.

All do well in Spain given the correct treatment. Some, such as the Madonna lily, survive and bloom in Spanish villages on hot, windy roof-tops, and still look beautiful.

How to Grow Lilies: Deep, well-drained, rich soil with plenty of compost grows the best lilies. If your soil is too heavy or too light, bring it to the correct balance by adding organic matter in the form of peat, ground bark or sawdust.

See that the soil is damp all the year round. Lilies never quite stop growing, and so have no completely dormant period.

You can ease up on the watering when the leaves turn yellow, but the roots still need to be kept moist.

Dig a generous planting hole, 20-50 cm. deeper than the depth of the bulb, then put enough soil in the bottom to bring it up to the preferred level of each type of bulb.

The rule of thumb is to cover smaller bulbs with 5-7 cm. of soil, medium-sized bulbs with 7-10 cm. and big bulbs with 10-15 cm. of earth. You don't have to worry too much about the exact depth. Lilies have miracle roots — called contractile roots — which draw them down to the correct depth. It's better to plant too near the surface than too deeply.

Madonna lilies are an exception. Never cover them with more than 2 cm. of soil.

Space the bulbs 30 cm. apart. After planting (spread the roots out well) give a thorough watering and then cover with a mulch of grass clippings, compost or spent mushroom compost, which should be damp, or dampened after you put it on. This helps to keep the roots cool. The lilies will bloom better in dappled shade.

Lilies grow well in containers. Repot in late autumn or early spring.

Again Madonna lilies are the exception: plant or repot them in August.

A Specially Spanish Lily — Sea Daffodil

The wild, white sea daffodil grows out of the bare sand and flowers in July and August round the Spanish Mediterranean coast. Formerly common, it is now becoming rarer as building development covers its chosen sites.

The strap-shaped leaves look like the daffodil's and the flower is much the same, but with more open, spidery petals and an exotic fragrance.

When the flower dies, the oval seed-pod swells and finally splits to shed two black, glossy seeds. To get enough moisture during the long, hot summer, the big bulb lies deep. When grown in the garden, and given some water during the active period, it can be planted at 15-25 cm. deep in porous soil. Split clumps occasionally. Plant in full sun.

Tulips

Although the highly-bred Dutch tulips prefer a colder winter climate than that of coastal Spain, the wild tulips, often referred to as the *tulipa* species, occur naturally all round the Mediterranean, including southern Spain.

Many small-flowered, low-growing species are available. Some, such as the *praestans fusilier,* produce two to four tulips on each stem, in this case a vivid red.

The Lady tulip, *clusiana,* with its bi-coloured flowers (red on the outside and white inside) does particularly well in warm winter areas, as does the scented *tulipa saxatilis* whose lilac flowers with yellow bases grow up to three on each 30-cm. stem.

Plant these tulips in normal garden soil two and a half times as deep as they are wide. They can be left undisturbed for years and will form a colony. The only precaution to take is to pick off the dead flowers and stems as they fade, and cut off at ground level and remove the plant when it has turned yellow. This is important to prevent disease.

PARSLEY ROSEMARY SPEARMINT THYME OREGANO BASIL MARJORAM

An Alphabet of Herbs

ROM ancient times herbs have been valued both for their me-
dicinal and flavouring qualities. They have been surrounded
by an aromatic aura of mystery and enchantment, yet few
plants have a wider range of practical uses.

Herbs are chiefly used in cooking, where they are invaluable for en-
hancing the flavour of otherwise simple food. Special varieties can be
highly decorative, such as a pair of bay trees standing on each side of a
doorway. Some can be used as edging or hedging in the garden, others
have foliage valuable in flower arrangement.

Knowledge about the seasoning of food goes back thousands of years,
and ancient peoples had detailed information concerning the curative
powers of herbs. From Pedanius Dioscorides, personal physician to the

Emperor Nero, to Jesse Boot, the orphan boy who scoured the country-side for herbs and finally became the millionaire owner of a chain of chemist shops, herbs have been valued for the part they can play in promoting good health.

As so many herbs originally came from the Mediterranean area they grow particularly well in Spain, and a fully-stocked herb garden is a valuable asset. Plant it near the kitchen door where fresh sprigs can be picked easily. Make narrow beds beside paths (easy to reach in wet weather) and try to find a private, rather than a public place. In spring, a newly-planted herb garden is a pleasure to look at, but as the season wears on, some plants grow over-exuberant.

If you haven't room for a full herb garden, there are many decorative kinds — basil, bay, chives, parsley, sage, rosemary and thyme for instance — which can lead a double life as border plants. Many also do well in containers.

In the unlikely event of pests occurring in your herb garden, spray with a solution of Green Fairy Liquid (pure soap) and water. Should further treatment be needed use an insecticide such as Bayer's Baytroid, which contains one of the newer water-soluble insecticides, Piretroide. It is available in Spain.

Warning: Don't eat seeds from garden shops. These are planned for planting only and are sometimes pre-treated with chemicals, helpful for growth but not advisable for human consumption.

Kitchen and Aromatic Herbs and How to Grow Them

Angelica — a tall biennial which will grow to 200-250 cm. Both roots and leaves reduce the acidity of any fresh foods they are cooked with. The candied, green young flower-stems make a good decoration for cakes, and the leaves, fresh or dried, make a pleasant herb tea. Grow from root-division or seed. See that seed is fresh as it quickly loses its viability. Plant 45 cm. apart in a shaded place. Harvest stalks at the end of spring, and leaves before flowering.

Balm — a perennial with lemon-scented, heart-shaped leaves, said to ward off the physical effects of old age. About 50 cm. tall, it grows well from seed or can be propagated from cuttings and root-divisions. Plant or sow in spring. Use rich soil and don't over-water. Makes an excellent herb tea and enhances fish and chicken. Use also in salads and drinks in hot weather. A superb salad dressing is made of oil, lemon juice, lemon balm and sugar.

Basil — an annual, with leaves of varying shades of green and purple. Sow seeds in early spring. They germinate quickly but don't like being transplanted. If you must transplant, wait until the seedlings have firm bases and then lift them, keeping the roots covered with soil. Evening is a good time for this. Cook with tomatoes or pizzas and use raw in salads and sandwiches. Pleasant and spicy to taste, basil is often prized as a soother of jittery nerves.

Bay — not to be confused with the English laurel, this evergreen shrub is best bought from a nursery garden. If grown in a container, see that the soil does not dry out and spray the leaves occasionally with clear water. Bay possesses a marked flavour and half a leaf often gives the right balance as part of the classic bouquet garni.

Borage — an easy-to-grow annual. Sow seeds in spring. Chop the young, cucumber-flavoured leaves in salads, or use sprigs as a topping for Pimm's or other wine-cups. The brilliant blue flowers are also edible and most decorative. All parts of the plant are said to give a feeling of well-being.

Salad Burnet — a valuable perennial salad herb coming from the Mediterranean region, it was grown in England from the 16th century and taken to America by the Pilgrim Fathers. Sow seeds in spring and cover lightly with soil. For a constant supply of fresh leaves, cut the plants back, starting when the flower shoots appear. Grow in sun in poor soil with adequate water and good drainage. Never crop the plant by more than half. Can also be propagated by annual division of roots. An attractive, bushy plant growing about 25 cm. high, it does well in containers, and is a good addition to salads, vinegar and cream cheese.

Caraway — sow the seeds of this 60-cm. biennial in rich compost in late spring and never transplant. Don't worry if it is slow to germinate. Pay special attention to watering in the first year. The flowers and seeds will come the following summer. Use in cakes, on buns and mixed with cream cheese.

Chervil — an annual whose leaves have a light aniseed flavour, it makes a good addition to the traditional French *fines herbes*. Try it with roasts, casseroles and fish dishes. Grow in a shady spot.

Chilli — sow seeds in spring at a temperature of 18-21 °C. Prick out singly into pots and then plant out or pot as necessary. Use in curries, *chilli con carne* and chilli vinegar, which is made from green fruits before they turn colour. Full of vitamins. Dried berries last for months.

Fresh chillies keep well if put in a jar of salt moistened with water.

Chives — this delicate-flavoured member of the onion family grows well from seed sown in spring or from the division of roots. Garlic chives and the new F_1 hybrid Fruhlau are popular, the first for their flavour, and the second because they are very much earlier and more productive than the standard variety. Grow in a cool, sheltered place, keep moist and fertilize occasionally to compensate for continual cropping. Pick off flower buds for maximum crop. Chop the green "grass" for flavouring and decoration. All of the onion tribe contain very good quantities of vitamin C and trace elements which are said to reduce high blood pressure. Their phosphorous content is particularly recommended as an aid to lucid thinking, creativity, concentration and memory.

Comfrey — the common name, Knitbone, reflects the enormous reputation this herb had in times past for healing wounds and broken bones. However, the leaves have been found to contain a poison, and therefore no concoction of comfrey should be used internally. Nevertheless, ointments and poultices made from the leaves and roots can be used to treat rheumatism, arthritis, bruises and swellings. Comfrey is one of the very few plants which contain vitamin B_{12} (normally found in raw liver and egg), and also vitamins A, C, E, and the B complex group. Comfrey is a deep-rooted perennial and will grow in sun or partial shade. In warmer areas of Spain the leaves grow all year round. Elsewhere the plants are dormant in cold weather. To increase leaf production, remove flowering stalks and mulch with compost each spring. Grow from seed or root cuttings.

Coriander — an annual grown for its spicy seeds used in curries and casseroles. The flat leaf, which somewhat resembles parsley, is also known as Chinese or Mexican parsley. Used fresh, the herb has a pungent aroma and is much used in Moroccan, Indian, Chinese and Mexican cookery. Grow from seed in early spring, soaking the seed overnight. Give a rich, moist soil. Coriander dislikes being moved.

Cumin — a low-growing annual plant. The ground seeds are an essential part of curry powders. Grow from seed sown in early spring in rich loam in a well-drained, sunny position. It will mature in three to four months. Keep well watered as the plant cannot survive arid conditions.

Dill — an annual. Grow from seed any time in spring and don't transplant. Expect a height of 50 cm. Soothing to the digestion and good with cucumber. Use both leaves and seeds in yoghurt, salads, sauces and soups. Makes a good herb vinegar and the herb tea is a soothing nightcap.

Fennel — a perennial with fine, feathery leaves. Their smell is strong but nevertheless they make food taste delicious. Sow seeds in spring and be prepared for a height of 120 cm. The seed soon loses its viability so always buy fresh. Basal shoots will also grow if kept moist. Never allow fennel to flower.

Florence Fennel — a bulb-producing annual. Sow seed outdoors in spring, reducing plants to 15 cm. apart. The whole plant may be braised, stewed, used raw in salads, or the leaves used for flavouring. Try the improved Florence fennel "Sirio", an Italian-bred, rapid-growing variety which produces large, white, solid bulbs on compact plants. Sow seed in June for use in early autumn.

Feverfew — a hardy perennial of the daisy family, this herb is famous for its alleged ability to relieve headaches and migraine. Keep out of the strongest midday sunshine and do not allow to dry out. Either dry the leaves for use as herb tea or eat three or four leaves daily in a sandwich.

Garlic — the easy-to-grow "king" of herbs. Plant the cloves (bulb sections) in December leaving the tips at soil level, and spacing 15 cm. apart. Lift when the leaves turn yellow, dry in the sun and hang bunches in an airy place for winter use.

Ginger — the "bulb" with its thin, pale skin looking rather like a new potato, is in fact a swollen, horizontal stem. Will grow well in pots in sandy soil, but keep it out of the sun and give plenty of water during the summer. Green shoots appear in June. You can dig up the "root", cut off a piece for use in dishes such as curry, and then replant, sealing the cut with a dusting of sand. In the mountains bring the pot into shelter in November. Never water during cold weather.

Horseradish — use the root only and don't attempt to eat the leaves. The root stimulates appetite and digestion and is rich in vitamin C. Traditionally used as a relish with beef and surprisingly good with tomato soup. Likes deeply-dug, rich soil. Will grow in a container but needs a depth of 60 cm. Plant 7-cm. root cuttings in February or March.

Hyssop — an easy perennial herb growing to about 50 cm. tall. It is one of the herbs of the old monastery gardens of medieval Europe and is useful as a flavouring for rich meats such as pork, as it helps aid the digestion of fat. Today, perhaps a more important role is as a companion plant for brassica, helping to avoid club-root: hyssop is disliked by the Cabbage White butterfly. Propagate by seed, cuttings or the division of roots.

Lemon Grass — a perennial with leaves which have a lemon-like scent and flavour. It grows well in warm gardens but never flowers. In cultivation for centuries, the base, stem and sometimes leaves are used for flavouring, and it is an important ingredient in Eastern and North African dishes. Propagate by the division of an existing clump.

Lovage — a tall perennial plant which grows to a metre or more high and takes three or four years to reach full size. It is one of the most useful herbs. Its name refers to love, as it is said to give an all-pervading feeling of well-being. Use it to flavour savoury dishes and soups, but use with discretion as the flavour is strong. An infusion of chopped lovage leaves, either fresh or dried, makes a tisane which stimulates the digestion. Propagate by seeds sown in autumn or by root-division in spring. Seeds prefer low temperatures and darkness for germination. Later plant out allowing 45 cm. each way. Keep well watered. One or two specimens of this large plant will serve the needs of a family. Additional uses: the young stalks can be blanched and eaten like celery or candied for decoration as with angelica.

Marjoram — an easy-to-grow perennial. Sow seeds in early spring or take rooted shoots from an established plant. It is invaluable in a bouquet garni, stews, stuffings, tomato dishes and with eggs. Marjoram likes well-drained soil, and water in hot weather. Harvest leaves before the plant flowers.

Sweet Marjoram — an annual growing to 25 cm., whose name derives from Greek, meaning "joy of the mountains". The flavour is mild, sweet and delicious, and is at its best rubbed on joints of meat or poultry. Herbalists recommend sweet marjoram to alleviate depression and to treat high blood pressure, headaches and neuralgia. Sow seeds in spring.

Mint — there are many varieties, including the rare, white-splashed Gibraltar mint, but all do better with moisture and some shade. Aromatic, cool, sweet and fresh, mint is easy to grow and may sometimes have to be restrained from invading other plants. Grow from a root or from seed. Cutting helps fresh growth and the plant should never be allowed to flower. Cut down to the ground between October and November and again in spring after the new growth matures, to get the maximum crop of fresh, green shoots. If you want an uninterrupted supply, cut back half the crop and the other half three weeks later. Then cover with a mulch of compost.

Replace mint.in pots every two years and in the garden every three years. New plants form easily from cuttings rooted in water or lift old plants and discard all but the new outer shoots.

Myrrh — otherwise known as sweet cicely. This graceful perennial herb grows up to one metre tall, with delicate lacy green leaves. Grow it in shade or semi-shade, in good, well-drained soil kept moist. Seeds planted in autumn produce seedlings in spring. Can be propagated by root-division. Add chopped stems to desserts, fruit salads and delicate soups for their sweet anise flavour. Bees love the scent of the early summer white flowers.

Nasturtium — an easy annual with bold, bright flowers, nasturtiums originally came from Peru and were first introduced to Europe in 1574 when seeds were brought to Spain. Nasturtiums in all their varieties have a high vitamin C content in the leaves. The spicy, peppery flavour is helpful to anyone on a diet which restricts the intake of salt and pepper. Chop leaves and flowers and add to salads, sandwiches or cream cheese (just before serving). Sow seed in spring or autumn.

Oregano — marjoram and oregano are both varieties of the same plant and taste very much alike. It is sometimes possible to find trailing oregano which has a more prostrate habit than the common variety and can be grown cascading down a wall. Keep plants well trimmed to prevent flowering and the formation of woody growth. Propagate by seeds sown in early spring or by root cuttings.

Parsley — this famous biennial herb rich in iron and vitamin C, is said to be the basis of many remedies administered by the medieval monks. It prefers shade or semi-shade, a light, rich soil and moisture. Sow seeds from spring to midsummer in rows 30 cm. apart and thin plants to 15 cm. apart. Pick leaves from the outside of the clump not from the centre.

Poppy Seeds — edible poppy seeds come from the opium poppy, although the seeds themselves don't contain the drug. This annual poppy with its bluish-green leaves looks attractive in the garden. Scatter the seeds on the soil and cover with a light sprinkling of sand. Cut the seed-heads just before they turn from green to brown and leave them to dry in a light place until the seeds fall out.

Rosemary — a perennial, aromatic shrub which grows easily from cuttings and also makes attractive low hedges. Prune lightly occasionally to prevent woody growth. Cook a sprig or two with roast meats. It is safe to use wild rosemary as their are no poisonous varieties.

Saffron — comes from the Eastern Mediterranean, and today Spain is one of the largest growers in the world. The spice, with its yellow colour and distinctive flavour, is derived from the stigmas of a special, pinkish-purple perennial autumn crocus. Although like in appearance to some other autumn crocuses, it is essential to use only the correct variety *Crocus sativus.* The cost of saffron production is extremely high as the stigmas are picked by hand, and it takes 150,000 flowers to produce one kilo.

The corms grow best in rich, sandy but well-drained soil in a sheltered place. Plant the corms in August. As soon as the flowers open in autumn, harvest them and pick out the stigmas. Dry them at once, either in the sun or on sieves over a low heat. When dry, store at once in an airtight container. Increase by division of clumps. It is sometimes possible to get seed.

Sage — a famous perennial herb with leaves which are an aid to the digestion of rich meat such as pork and duck. Also excellent with onions, fish, cheese and liver, sage will grow either from root divisions or from seed. Plant in well-drained soil and keep watered in summer.

Summer Savory — an annual used in stuffings and pork dishes, and to enhance casseroles, white fish and soups. Sow seed in the open garden in spring. Don't transplant.

Winter Savory — a perennial, native to the dry, rocky places of southern Europe. Excellent in minced meat, stews, stuffings and salads. Also makes an interesting "mint" sauce. Sow seed in spring or grow from a cutting with a "heel" attached. When established, trim to encourage new growth and feed by covering the surface of the soil with a little rich earth. Water, but don't dig the new soil in.

Sorrel — a hardy perennial growing about 30 cm. high. The tangy, lemon-flavoured leaves are a piquant addition to soups, salads and omelettes. An ancient remedy, herbalists claimed that it flushed out poisons from the system caused by illness or alcohol. Very easy to grow, sorrel will stand up to cold in mountain gardens. Grow from seed or divide roots in spring or autumn. Plant in semi-shade and water well. Cut flowers to prevent the formation of seeds and replace old plants every four years. Sorrel grows quickly and will provide leaves three to four months after a spring sowing.

Sesame Seed — an annual which comes from tropical countries. Sow seeds at the end of summer when the foxglove-like flowers ripen, or in March, in the open garden. The seeds have a high vitamin content and should be lightly fried to reduce their size before being scattered on breads, cakes, rolls and biscuits. They also add an interesting nutty flavour to egg dishes.

Tarragon — not a herb to raise from seed as it is essential to get French tarragon — a very special hybrid which does not produce seed — as opposed to Russian tarragon. Buy an established plant if possible, or try a root cutting planted in spring. Cherish this beautiful herb in a sheltered place in well-drained soil. Tarragon makes one of the best herb vinegars.

Thyme — a component of the traditional French bouquet garni. Sow the seeds of this perennial plant in spring. Even better and with a more delicate flavour is lemon thyme. Sow seed also in spring in a sunny, well-drained place and feed occasionally with liquid fertilizer. Don't over-water.

Container Herbs

Balm, bay, basil, chervil, chives, chilli, coriander, fennel, feverfew, garlic (for leaves only), ginger, horseradish (use a deep container), marjoram, mint, parsley, poppy seeds, rosemary, sage, tarragon and thyme, will all grow in pots.

How To Dry Herbs

Pick just before the plants flower — except when seeds are needed — and hang in a ventilated room in small bunches. If possible, don't use artificial heat, and avoid direct sunlight. When dry, crumble and store in jars.

In the Freezer: Chives contain a high proportion of moisture, so seal in small plastic containers and quick freeze-dry them.

To Make Herb Butter

Mix two tablespoons of fresh, chopped herbs with 100 grams of softened butter and a pinch of cayenne pepper or celery salt. With wet hands, shape the butter into a roll 3 cm. in diameter. Wrap the butter in foil, seal in a polythene bag and freeze. To serve: unwrap the frozen butter and cut into slices using a knife dipped in hot water, or allow to soften and fill small pots.

To Make Herb Vinegar

Pick herbs just before they flower and cover the leaves with double their volume of warm wine vinegar. Allow to stand, covered, until you get the flavour you want — anything from two weeks to two months — then strain through a plastic sieve or muslin into clean bottles.

For decoration, poke in a spray or two of the herbs used before you cork or seal. This won't alter the flavour but looks attractive. Store in a cool, dark place. If using screw-top metal lids, first cover the mouth of the jars with plastic wrap.

Garlic Vinegar: Use three cloves of garlic, skinned and coarsely chopped, and 500 ml (approx 1 pint) of wine vinegar. Put the garlic in a warmed jar. Bring the vinegar to the boil and pour it on to the garlic. Cool and cover. Leave for a week, then strain and bottle.

Horseradish Vinegar: Use 40 grams of grated horseradish to each 500 ml of vinegar.

Chilli Vinegar: Use 25 grams of crushed chillies to 500 ml of vinegar.

Herb Drinks

For mint and other herb teas take a good handful of leaves, pour on boiling water and allow to stand for 6-7 minutes. Dried leaves make a rather stronger tea than fresh.

Lawns — How to
Make and Maintain

 VERY garden needs a lawn," is an opinion widely held among gardeners. But how that lawn is to be planned and the type of grass used, are decisions for each individual, according to site, family needs and budget.

Planning Your Lawn

A lawn looks its best close to the house, giving a sense of space, a green contrast to bright flowers and an immediate invitation to stroll out into the garden. But in Spain grass needs plenty of water, and continual flooding is bad for the foundation of a building. So link your house and garden with a terrace. In this way you can have a fine lawn and a home with foundations unimpaired.

Next, consider where the main wear will occur. Perhaps it will be the route to the swimming pool or a cut across the grass to the tennis court. Plan a path to carry the traffic. It's impossible to keep any kind of grass looking good under continuous heavy wear.

For best results, plant your new lawn in April or October.

Choose the Right Grass
Consider your land and your life objectively. What type of grass will grow well on the site? What is your budget? How much time are you willing to spend on lawn care and what are your needs?

A luxury lawn grown with an expensive grass such as the popular Cape Royal or Bermuda Grass, looks magnificent when in perfect condition, but even when given every attention this grass will not do well if close to the coast and exposed to a salty, east *levante* wind.

An expensive, pedigree lawn needs a constant supply of water in the summer and regular weekly mowing — and it won't welcome the rough and tumble of life with children.

For a hard-wearing, easy-care, budget lawn use the widely popular *grama,* which is planted sprig by sprig.

Cut up a square of *grama* turf into small sprigs or stolons. Plant them 10 cm. apart and they will soon join up to form an attractive, easy-case sweep of grass. "A budget lawn that is well looked after is more attractive than an expensive one that is neglected" is the opinion among professional garden experts.

Once you have decided on the type and layout you want, there are three main steps to ensure that your lawn will give you lasting satisfaction.

Clearing the Site
First clear the site of all existing vegetation, roots and stones. Then dig the land over thoroughly to reduce the soil to a fine tilth. It is important to see that the fertile topsoil remains on top and that no subsoil is brought to the surface. If you have less than 15 cm. of topsoil, either all over or in any part, buy more from a nursery garden to make up the necessary all-over depth to 15 cm.

At this stage work in granulated peat or well-rotted manure or compost at four kilos per square metre. This will make the soil more moisture-retentive, which is a great help to the lawn during hot weather.

For a large lawn, underground water-pipes with fittings for sprinklers are a great convenience. Lay them now.

Smoothing the Surface
Rake the surface well until it is smooth, fine in tilth and free from high

and low spots. A successful lawn may slope gently but should be free from bumps and hollows. Water it well, then when nearly dry, roll it in two directions with a garden roller. Finally check the levels again, and adjust if necessary.

Sowing Seed or Planting Stolons

Before making a final choice of the type of grass for a new lawn, discuss the matter with a nursery gardener. He will know the area and the types of grass which do best there. You may even need different grasses in different parts of the garden — one type for the main lawn and another to stabilize a bank, for instance. For banks, look out for *Festuca Rubra Estolonifera.* This is a good, heavy-duty grass often used for playing fields. Owing to its root formation it is excellent for preventing soil-slip in steep places. Allow 15-20 grams per square metre.

Choose a day when the surface of the soil is dry on top but moist beneath. Buy enough seed to provide 50 grams per square metre and divide it into four parts. Sow by hand one quarter of the seed up the lawn, one quarter down the lawn, one quarter from left to right and one quarter from right to left. This ensures an even distribution. If you have a seed distributor the work can be done in two stages only, sowing half the seed across and the other half up and down the site.

Finally, rake the whole area with a wire rake to cover the seed. If birds are a nuisance, criss-cross the area with black cotton, 10 cm. above the ground.

When planting stolons, pre-soak the bed and let it dry out to a good working consistency. Make a series of parallel trenches 7 cm. deep and 10 cm. apart. Plant the stolons vertically in the trenches at 10-cm. intervals, pressing back the soil as you go. Work as fast as possible to prevent the stolons drying out and keep reserve supplies protected from wind and sunlight.

After-Care
When the seedlings are 5 cm. high or the stolons well established, the new lawn is ready for its first cut. Set the blades of the mower high and see that they are oiled and sharp.

From now on, mow regularly but lightly, reducing the height of the blades gradually until the turf is closely knit. Never let the new lawn get completely dry. Sprinklers are a convenient method of irrigation, and are better used in the morning or evening, avoiding the hours of hottest sun.

Caring for An Existing Lawn
A fine lawn can be kept in good order or a poor lawn repaired by sensible attention. Both evaporation and mowing remove a great deal of moisture from the grass, and this must be replaced regularly.

A thorough soaking down to the bottom of the roots twice a week is of far more value than a continual light sprinkling.

Lift a small square of turf and you will be able to see if the water is penetrating the full depth of the root system. Adjust your watering accordingly.

Top Dressing
In spring every lawn responds to the tonic of a good top dressing. Give a light application of granulated peat mixed with coarse river sand in equal quantities, and brush the mixture into the roots. Normally the spring rain will be enough to water the dressing in, but if no rain has fallen in four or five days use hose or sprinklers.

Feeding
All plants need feeding but grass more than most, to compensate for the heavy losses sustained by mowing.

About four weeks after top dressing with peat and sand, apply another top dressing of sulphate of ammonia or a proprietary fertilizer such as "Quince-Quince-Quince", so-called because it contains 15 per cent nitrogen, 15 per cent phosphoric acid and 15 per cent potassium.

Use sulphate of ammonia at one and a quarter kilos per 100 square metres, and proprietary brands according to the instructions given on the packet.

It is important to apply fertilizer evenly, as too great a concentration in one place can damage the lawn. For even distribution apply a strip one metre wide all round the edge of the grass. Then divide the remaining material into two equal parts, and distribute half up and down the lawn, and the other half from side to side. For even better results, give another feed in early autumn.

Weeding

In a lawn made of ordinary *grama* grass, regularly mown, weeds present little problem, but fine lawns may be invaded either by weeds or the strong-growing *grama*. Spray the intruder with the weed-killer "Round-Up" (known in England as "Tumbleweed"). This Bayer product is made in Spain and is highly effective. Later, dig out the dead growth, add more soil and re-seed or plant new stolons of the grass of your choice.

Problem Areas

Bumps and hollows are dealt with by cutting the turf in an "H" formation with the centre bar of the "H" running through the affected area. Then roll back the turf exposing the problem. For bumps, remove the topsoil, lower the level of the subsoil, replace the topsoil and relay the turf.

For hollows, simply add enough topsoil to rectify the level and replace the turf.

Broken edges: Make the repair by cutting out the affected area in rectangular turfs and switching them round so that a sound portion is on the edge. Re-sow the small broken area.

What Went Wrong?

Well cared for lawns in Spain suffer from virtually no diseases, but occasionally unexpected problems arise.

Brown spots in an otherwise healthy lawn may result from several causes: machine oil may have dripped on to the grass while the mower was being serviced; there may be builders' rubble buried shallowly beneath the surface so that the grass hasn't enough rich soil to feed on; a bitch may have access to the lawn, or too much fertilizer may have been applied to one place. Once identified, these problems are easily dealt with by the removal of the cause.

Herb Lawns

Aromatic lawns for very light use can be made of herbs. One of the easiest types to grow in Spain is the thyme lawn. For this, use the smallest variety *(Thymus serpyllum)*, which has an attractive scent when crushed.

Sow seed in spring. Water well and weed carefully until the plants have matted together, and continue watering throughout the dry season.

Pennyroyal *(Mentha pulegium)*, grows up to 30 cm. high, but by occasional clipping or mowing it can be kept to 12 cm. Water well and feed occasionally. It is a good creeping plant and prefers partial shade. Increase by summer cuttings in moist soil, spraying the young plants well to prevent drying out. Alternatively, divide in spring.

The low-growing Corsican mint, native of Corsica and Sardinia, with its pale mauve, summer flowers, may be clipped once or twice a year to keep the lawn low and close to the ground.

For heavier use, plant camomile. In its variety *Anthemis nobilis* it makes a fragrant and useful lawn which will stand as much wear as grass. Part of the lawns at Buckingham Palace are planted with camomile. Sow seeds in boxes or seed-beds in spring and transplant when seedlings are large enough to handle. Or buy plants in spring or autumn and plant 10 cm. apart. To get a thick lawn, mow lightly but regularly in late spring and summer to prevent flowering, starting when the plants are 7 cm. high.

Trees

REES have the advantage that they take their place in the garden comparatively quickly and give pleasure for a long time.

They give a sense of permanence, and can provide shade, year-round colour, and privacy from the outside world.

They are valuable both for the beauty of their shapes and for their contrasting forms and colours. Yuccas with their great spikes set off the tall distinction of Norfolk Island pines; fluffy, yellow mimosas are a foil for sturdy, broad conifers. A world of variety is available through trees.

Anyone who has seen the picture of Winston Churchill in his garden at Chartwell — plump back bowed in total despair — sitting on the stump of a favourite tree which his wife Clemmie had had felled while he was away, understands the feeling people have for trees.

Affection grows with the tree. If it is large, you love it for its permanence. If it is small and new, you love it because you have planted it yourself.

Spain grows so many different and beautiful trees that gardeners new to the subtropical climate may be tempted to believe that they can grow anything here. But in the same way as some tender plants won't grow in northern climates, some trees have a "cold weather requirement" and won't thrive by the Mediterranean. The lilac is one example. So when choosing a tree, make sure that it will grow well in your particular garden.

Another point to think about is the availability of water. Normally a tree will look after itself when the first two or three years have passed; but in the early stages you will have to water it, until the roots have grown large enough to find moisture for themselves.

Choosing and Siting

Now you have to decide what trees to choose and where you are going to put them.

Keep plantings well away from the house unless you need shade. A traditional Spanish villa often has two or three palm trees shading the back terrace where the family sits in summer in the heat of the day. Otherwise plant trees where you can easily see their differing colours and shapes.

For a small garden one has to exercise discipline: not too many trees or it will become a jungle. A good selection might be a group of three palm trees and two yuccas. An uneven number is effective.

Even in a small garden try to squeeze in a couple of mimosas. The more restricted your space, the more important it is to make the right choice.

For one, choose the variety *dealbata* which flowers in the winter. For the other plant a mimosa *floribunda* which comes out in waves of fluffy, yellow-scented blossom several times a year. With more space available you can plan a more ample strategy. Contrast will accentuate the delicate, pale green and mourning shape of a weeping willow, set near the portly mass of a conifer such as *Leylandii*. Give it plenty of water.

The red leaves of a prunus lighten an over-green picture for most of the year, and white blossom covers its bare branches in January.

A Norfolk Island pine with its distinctive, upswept branches will grow into a landmark.

A plane tree is also distinctive with its large, five-pointed leaves and fine, mottled trunk. It has the disadvantage, however, that the leaves fall every autumn in a thick carpet. Either rake them up, or site the tree in the hinterland of your garden where the litter doesn't matter.

If you have a skyline to adorn but not obscure — or any other open space — plant the narrowly upright Italian cypress, either singly or in a file. Don't group them. It is the dark columns pointing upwards which give them their outstanding personality. Once established they last a lifetime, needing no attention at all.

The Judas Tree is so-named because by tradition it is the tree on which Judas hanged himself. The Spanish have chosen a gentler name, they call it the tree of love, perhaps because each spring it is smothered with purplish-pink flowers.

For a beautiful and most unusual tree plant the Maidenhair tree, named in the east, ginkgo. It has been called a "living fossil" as it is the only member of its tribe left in the world. It needs a long summer to ripen the wood and should do well in Spanish gardens.

The main attraction of the ginkgo is its foliage. Infinitely small compared with the total size of the tree, each lime-green leaf is like a tiny frond of Maidenhair fern. When autumn comes, suddenly it is a glowing gold, as though it had burst into blossom.

The Maidenhair is a long-lived tree, but strangely enough it grows remarkably quickly from seed, reaching a height of about one metre in 18 months.

To grow from seed, place seeds in the freezer for two or three weeks as soon as they arrive to simulate the treatment that nature would hand out in less fortunate climates. This breaks the dormancy in the seed and tells it that it is time to grow. Then sow at once just below the surface of the soil. Firm down well and ideally maintain a temperature of 15-20 °C.

Other Trees to Choose

Almond — If possible find room for an almond tree for the pleasure of the sudden burst of bloom around the end of January. You can, like the Japanese, grow for the blossom alone, cutting the branches for home decoration. (Bring in the blossom when in bud and it will open early in a vase of water.)

If you want to harvest a crop of almonds as well, consult your nursery gardener about the varieties to plant. In most cases two varieties are needed for pollination. If you are short of room, plant two or three different kinds in one hole.

When the fruit comes — it looks like an undersized, dark green peach — remove the flesh and spread out the stones in the sun for a day or two to dry. To test when they are ready to store, shake the nuts. The kernels should rattle in the shells.

Almonds will survive on less water than most other fruit trees.

Bottle-Brush Tree — Callistemon — one of the most popular and colourful small trees to reach Spain from Australia. The rich crimson "bottle-brushes" which appear in summer are airy and eye-catching, and are followed by strange, woody capsules which look like beads pressed into the bark. Bottle-brushes love the sun and will stand up to most soils. There is also a white variety, but for maximum impact plant the red.

Eucalyptus — Here I feel I must declare an interest. I am a eucalyptus fan. I never drive in from the glare of the street into the shade of the tall eucalyptus trees without being thankful for the cool privacy they afford. In addition, eucalyptus grows in a beautiful tall shape, has narrow, hanging foliage, a non-aggressive but pervasive, aromatic tang and an attractive, mottled bark.

There are points to take into consideration. Eucalyptus grows quickly and may need pruning every 10-15 years if overhanging a driveway, to prevent damage from possible broken boughs when winds are high.

It is said that wide-ranging roots may damage building foundations. Plant not less than six metres from your walls, or set a tree in the garden well away from the house.

When buying, choose a small eucalyptus tree. It will soon grow, and transplants better at an early stage.

False Pepper Tree — Schinus. The evergreen, feathery leaves of the false pepper tree make an attractive feature for shade and interest. The elderly Spanish gentleman who first walked me some little distance to inspect a fine specimen growing at the other end of his village, warned me that the peppers — berries like peppercorns — are *not* to be eaten.

This attractive tree is available in many nurseries and will grow quickly, reaching a final height of three to four metres. Once established it can get by on little water. Don't plant too near the walls of your house. Both tree and roots need living room. Bear this in mind and the false pepper tree will be both handsome to look at and a comfort to sit under, and will take very little trouble to look after.

Jacaranda — a beautiful, blue-flowering tree with feathery foliage, which has the attractive habit of blossoming in the *feria* season in high summer, adding to the gaiety. A mature tree will grow from three to four metres.

Underplant jacaranda with mandevilla, the white "king jasmine". Both flower at the same time with stunning results.

Magnolia — The splendid magnolia of Spain can be surprising to those of us who have memories of cold-climate magnolias flowering with upward-flaring blooms on the bare branches of early spring. The explanation is simple: the magnolias grown in northern climates come from China and other nearby countries. These are deciduous and fail to grow tall as they receive a severe check each winter.

The Spanish magnolia comes from Florida. It is an evergreen tree, *Magnolia grandiflora*, which, as it retains its leaves throughout the year, makes great progress.

It loves to grow on rather sandy soil, such as it finds in Florida. But the winds of Florida often hamper its growth. In the warmer parts of Spain it finds an ideal climate, and on occasions reaches a height of 25 metres. Unlike many others, this magnolia is tolerant of lime. Its huge buds open up into cup-shaped white blossoms the size of a grapefruit.

Magnolias like abundant moisture — indeed it is essential to supply it in their early years. When they mature they can often survive unaided, as by then the root system will have developed enough to reach down to the water-table beneath.

The name of these beautiful trees commemorates the French enthusiast M. Pierre Magnol, director of the botanical gardens at Montpellier at the beginning of the 18th century.

Magnolias are thought to be one of the oldest plants in the world, and fossilized remains have been found dated from over five million years ago.

The Rubber Tree has the Latin name *Ficus elastica* (rubber fig) because, rather surprisingly, it is a member of the fig family.

You can buy it in a florist's shop as a pot plant, and when it grows too big for the house, plant it out in the garden. Or you can buy the rubber tree already grown in many nurseries. A native of India and Malaya, it does exceptionally well in Spain. Its big, glossy, dark green leaves and pointed, crimson buds make it an interesting tree to watch. Remember that it may eventually grow tall, up to 12 metres with a spread of about half its height, so allow enough room for future development.

Sago Palm — Cycas — is not a true palm tree but a survivor from an ancient group which covered the earth a hundred million years ago, and later gave rise to the conifer family.

These unusual, eye-catching trees bear male and female flowers on separate plants and look like a cross between a palm and a fern.

Find it a place in the garden in full view, where its strange, short, thick trunk and burst of leathery, deeply-cut leaves at the top show up to full advantage. It may well form a primeval-looking clump of the utmost individuality. Give average water.

The Smoke Tree — Cotinus — has varieties native both to the USA and southern Europe. It has earned its name "smoke tree" on account of its curious inflorescences and fruiting bodies which are made up of an infinite number of filaments which change colour from pink and pale purple to grey.

This tree is often known as the Venetian Sumach (pronounced "Shoemack"), and a legendary anecdote links it with the writer J. M. Barrie, creator of the immortal Peter Pan.

Standing in front of a smoke tree, an opinionated gardener started to lecture Barrie on pronunciation.

"Sumach is the only word in the English language where 's' is pronounced 'sh'," he declared.

"Are you sure?" murmured Barrie.

Left to itself, the tree will grow to about five metres high and three or more metres wide. For considerations of space it can be kept to about two metres wide by shortening side-shoots in early spring back to two buds of the previous year's growth.

The cotinus is a deciduous tree, but from spring through to fall it is furnished with rounded leaves which burn with red and orange tints in autumn. Give it average to poor soil. Too much pampering results in growth at the expense of "smoke" and autumn colour.

Strawberry Tree — Arbutus — is an interesting tree native to the Mediterranean area, which is particularly valuable as it is a slow grower, and doesn't take up too much room. A bear leaning on an arbutus is the symbol of Spain's capital city, Madrid. The small, white bell-shaped flowers which come in autumn, are followed by clusters of round, red "strawberry" fruit. Excellent evergreen trees for hot, dry soils, as they need virtually no watering when established.

Coral Tree — Erythrina. Medium sized, with brilliant red blossom in early summer, the coral tree loves warmth, some water and good drainage. In cooler areas the height is reduced. Grow it in a pot and shelter indoors in a bright place in winter.

Laburnum — An attractive flowering tree covered with clusters of yellow pea-like blossoms in late spring. Best in gardens which are not too hot, where it should be sited in full sun. In warmer areas plant where shaded from hottest afternoon sunshine. Teach children not to eat the seeds, which are poisonous.

So many trees beautiful in foliage or flower grow in Spain, that no garden with trees need be without year-round interest.

Planting a Tree

Except in the case of trees planted from pots, deciduous trees should be planted in their dormant, or leafless stage, that is, between October and February, according to the season.

Container-grown trees can be transplanted with very little disturbance to the root-ball and so this can be done over a much longer season. Avoid only extremes of weather — bad weather in winter or heatwaves in summer.

Evergreens are usually planted in March, when new growth is starting and the plant is at its most vital. Again there is much greater latitude with container-grown specimens.

Right siting is of the utmost importance. Think how tall and wide your tree will grow and give it plenty of living room. Don't overcrowd — not as it is now, but as it will be in the future.

Spanish gardeners bear the question of water very much in mind when planting a tree.

First a good hole is dug. A capacity of a cubic metre will make a fine home for a fair-sized tree. Smaller trees can do with a little less room. Fork over the bottom of the hole and then add a layer of manure or compost. Cover it with a thin layer of soil as manure must never touch the roots.

Next, make a mound of good, rich earth in the bottom of the planting hole. Your garden soil will do nicely if it is in good condition. If not, buy a bag of good loam.

It takes two to plant a tree, one to support it and one to fill in the soil.

Spread out the roots comfortably over the mound, and see that the tree will finally be at the same level as it was in the nursery. Judge by the mark on the trunk.

Now insert the stake. You will be able to see where the roots are and avoid damaging them.

(It isn't always necessary to put in a stake. The trunk of the tree will thicken better without one. But unless your garden is really sheltered or the tree is short and broad, as are some conifers, be on the safe side and stake it. Until the tree is well established, check the tie two or three times a year to see that it is still secure and still large enough. Finally, remove the stake.)

Fill in the hole making sure that there are no air pockets. Tread the earth down gently but firmly. Tie the trunk to the stake with a soft, loose band, leaving room for a little movement.

Build a low retaining wall round the perimeter of the hole. Now water well. The retaining wall will prevent the water flooding away over the rest of the garden. Every drop will go down where it is needed to the roots below.

Once established, a tree usually needs little or no attention. But nurse it through the early years with careful watering and an annual top dressing of well-rooted manure or a fertilizer. A tree planted in grass should have a circle of soil left round it.

How long should this early special care continue? It varies with each individual planting. An old gardener once explained: "To begin with the roots have to get established. They may take their time. But all the while activity is going on underground. When the tree is ready it will start to grow."

To Prune an Ornamental Tree

On the whole for landscape trees, the less pruning that is done the better, but there are exceptions.

You may wish to improve the shape. For instance, shorten the branches of a young weeping willow back to a basic outline, and it will break out into a richer profusion of graceful, weeping branches.

Remove the lower fronds of a young palm tree each year to lengthen the trunk until the full height is reached, after that don't touch it. Be careful when pruning to maintain the trunk in the shape of a column. Don't over-prune and get a shape like the point of a pencil.

Tidy a mature yucca by removing the grey "beard" hanging below the new green leaves. Immediately it appears rejuvenated.

Prune to remove dead, damaged or diseased branches well back beyond the source of trouble. Do this as soon as you notice anything amiss.

Prune away branches that cross or are overcrowded. If possible, wait for the winter months.

Always use a sharp instrument, whether pruning-knife, secateurs, long-arm or saw. Cut cleanly at an angle, just above a healthy bud or leaf. See that the angle will direct rain to the ground, not back into the tree.

The reason for cutting above a bud or leaf is that the buds and leaves call sap into the branch. If there are no buds, no sap will come and the stump will die, possibly causing infection.

If a Tree Blows Over

If a storm causes a single-stemmed tree to blow over, such as a palm tree or a yucca, you may be able to salvage something from the wreck.

Saw the trunk up into lengths about one metre long and plant them. They may take root and reward you with a series of new trees.

Citrus

ERE in Spain citrus trees are a natural birthright, and can take their place in the ornamental garden, looking attractive in foliage, blossom and fruit.

All need fast-draining soil. If your garden can't supply this, plant citrus in a raised bed or in a container. Citrus need moist soil, but there must also be air in that soil, hence the need for good drainage.

The roots spread out twice as far as the distance from the trunk to the branch ends, so water widely, keeping the water off the trunk itself as much as possible.

Lemon

One of the most useful of all fruit trees is the lemon (legend says that Eve came out of the Garden of Eden hiding a lemon in her hand). Lemons grow excellently in Spain and several varieties are available at the *vivero*.

Buy more than one type of tree if you want a plentiful crop. These will fruit once or twice a year according to kind. Also, don't fail to plant one or two of the frailer Lunar lemons, which carry some blossom each month on their slender lateral branches, with the result that there are always some thin-skinned lemons ready for use.

All types of lemon share the same requirements: not too much water, so don't set them in a beautiful lawn where the sprinklers are always going; only prune when necessary to remove crossed branches and to allow light and air into the centre of the tree, and cut out strong, upward-growing shoots. The lemons are borne on the finer, lateral branches, so the crop will be larger if the tree is encouraged to produce more of these.

Finally, and this goes for all fruit trees, they will crop better if a circle of land is cultivated round them.

Grapefruit

Another member of the *Citrus* family, the grapefruit needs the same treatment as the lemon: not too much water and only prune when essential. "Just leave it to grow as it grows," a Spanish nursery gardener said. Expect a big tree eventually, up to seven metres tall.

Orange

The orange might be called the national fruit of Spain. Nothing could be easier to grow than the bitter Seville orange with its glossy, green leaves and beautiful, keen-scented blossom in spring. It is true that the fruit is only useful for making marmalade, but the tree is trouble-free, disease-free and decorative.

Sweet Oranges, Clementines and Mandarins

To grow sweet oranges successfully — also clementines and mandarins — spray three times a year against green mite and other invaders. "Dursban 48" is useful, available in one-litre bottles. Dilute 33 cc in one litre of water. Spray immediately after the crop is picked; thereafter at intervals of four months.

Prune young trees (bitter oranges too) to allow for at least one metre of trunk before allowing the branches to fan out.

Growing Citrus in Pots

Former British Prime Minister Sir Alec Douglas Home, was given an unknown but attractive little plant in a pot. It turned out to be a seedling orange tree.

"When I was given the tree it was only six inches high. I was very fond of it," he says.

It flourished in the drawing room of Sir Alec's home on the Scottish borders near Coldstream, and after three years came into flower and started to bear fruit. "I suppose we have had four hundred oranges from it," he estimates. "The fruit was very good and the tree gave off a very pleasant scent."

Finally, with the years the orange tree grew so large that it had to be given away, and now luxuriates in the benign climate of a butterfly farm near Edinburgh.

Orange: When grown in pots, orange trees have a special miniature charm. In a light place on the patio they can be a winter show-piece, with keenly-scented blossom followed first by dark green globes and later by the bright, mature fruit.

I have seen an orange tree only 40 cm. high standing in a pot on a patio ledge and bearing three full-sized oranges. Its charm lay in its very absurdity, so small, yet so self-important, as though it were in fact a real, full-sized orange tree.

Five years later it was a little over one metre high and was bearing 10 or 12 oranges each season. A dwarf version of the Valencia orange, the tree had never been repotted. It was watered regularly — more in summer, less in winter — fed once a month, and each spring given a top dressing of peat.

If you are buying from a nursery and can't find a dwarf variety — that is, one that has been grafted on to a dwarfing stock — there are many alternatives.

Look out for the Calamondin orange from the Philippines, which is small by nature, and bears white, sweetly-scented flowers for most of the year.

When well established, it will probably carry a load of half-ripe and ripe fruit together, while bearing at the same time a flush of blossom. Truly a conversation piece. The fruit isn't really up to eating quality, but you can make marmalade with it.

Clementine: The clementine is another attractive citrus plant for container growing. The white, fragrant blossom comes out late in spring and is followed by sweet, juicy, thin-skinned fruit.

Lemon: Lemon trees will also grow in pots. According to variety, the sweet-scented, white flowers appear at any time of year, often followed by an abundance of fruit. Don't worry if some drop as they develop. It's only nature's way of saying that the little tree is carrying more fruit than it can cope with.

Help your lemon tree by removing any suckers (extra shoots coming up independently from the soil), and prune to get a compact little tree with many twigs, rather than strongly-developed branches. It is on the twigs that the fruit is formed.

If you live in a part of Spain where patio temperatures are occasionally low in winter, the lemon will ride the drop with less trouble than other types of citrus.

Other Citrus Trees: In addition to sweet oranges, Seville oranges, blood oranges and navel oranges all make attractive patio plants.

Loose-skinned tangerines and the little satsumas are, by nature, compact and useful for growing in pots. The unusual citron is fun to have on the patio. You may even make your own candied peel from your citron, which is a nobbly-looking fruit, almost all skin and no pulp, and the commercial source of candied peel.

The lime is an interesting tree to possess. Its small, lemon-shaped, greenish fruit are a superb source of vitamin C (hence the name "Limeys" that Americans gave the English, since they drank lime juice to keep off scurvy on the long sea voyage across the Atlantic).

The lime will grow in a pot for many years. The fruit has a keen following of fans who say that the juice has a different and even better flavour than the lemon. Remember that lime trees are slightly more tender than lemon trees, but will be safe in a winter temperature down to 6 °C.

If you plan to grow grapefruit in a container, face up to the fact that eventually you will need a large pot or tub. This is an occasion when you can stop the main upward-leading shoot when you feel the tree is tall enough. The flowers appear on the tips of the shoots and have a strong scent.

Growing Your Own Trees from Cuttings and Pips

Cuttings: Try 10-cm. cuttings taken from young wood planted in sandy soil — either in small, individual pots or round the edge of a larger pot. Keep them out of the sun and in moist soil. Protection by surrounding plants gives a helpful micro-climate. Lemons respond particularly well to this treatment. Cover the pot with a polythene bag to encourage rooting.

Pips: Growing citrus from pips is a favourite method as it is very little trouble, and this makes any failures unimportant.

Take seeds from as fresh, ripe and juicy a fruit as you can find. Never let them dry out and pop them at once into moist, light soil. Be careful not to plant too deeply; about 1 cm. deep is best, as pips may have their emerging shoots distorted by having to push through too much soil.

This comparatively shallow planting means that you must watch carefully to see that the soil does not dry out. Making a mini-propagator by covering with a plastic bag is helpful, but even then check every few days that the soil is moist.

If you have a house-plant growing in light soil that is kept warm and moist, try tucking a pip into the same pot. When the shoot emerges transfer it to other quarters. Many successful citrus trees have been started off this way.

After-Care

There are a few rules to bear in mind for success when growing citrus in pots.

Don't disturb the roots except when repotting is essential.

Every year in early spring give a top dressing of fresh, good soil, removing a little of the existing earth in the pot if necessary.

Water fully and regularly, never in dribbles. If water comes through to the saucer below, throw it away.

Spray the leaves of your patio plant from time to time. It will refresh the little tree. Fertilize regularly.

There is no need to prune pot-grown citrus except to maintain the shape you need.

Growing citrus trees in pots is a fascinating hobby, always full of pleasant surprises. A dozen oranges hanging on a tree in a 30-cm. pot can give more pleasure than a sackful bought in the market.

Magnolia, a magnificent tree with its characteristic large flowers.
(Photo by AGE)

Palm Trees are a majestic feature of many Spanish gardens. (Photo by J. D. D.)

Hedges and Wind-Breaks

 EDGES play a quietly important part in the garden. They define boundaries, keep out intruders, provide privacy, give shelter from the wind, give relief from street dust and, within the garden itself, differentiate one area from another, adding to the pleasure of the whole.

There are varieties of hedge to suit many tastes and purposes, but the ground for most fine hedges needs the same sort of preparation.

Planting

A hedge will stay in place for a long time, so dig the ground deeply and well. Prepare the site in early spring, say, at the beginning of March, and plant after a short delay about the end of March or in April. You can also

113

plant a hedge in autumn. November is an excellent planting month.

The quickest way to get a good hedge is to plant two staggered rows close together. How close you should plant the hedging material depends on the size and nature of the individual bushes. Your supplier will be able to advise you.

Take out a trench at least one metre wide. If you have decided on a single hedge, for economy or any other reason, a trench 60 cm. wide will be enough.

It is important to dig the trench deeply and fill the bottom with rotted manure or compost. This encourages the roots to grow downwards and not quest out sideways, robbing nearby borders. Apart from top dressing, this original manuring is the only nourishment the hedge will ever have, so be generous now.

From the beginning, plan the final size and shape you want the hedge to be. This prevents mistakes, such as planting too near a wall or road.

Caring for Your Hedge

Tall hedges should be narrower at the top than at the bottom. If the hedge widens out at the top, the lower leaves and branches won't get enough light.

How often to clip or prune your hedge depends on its purpose, and the plants you have chosen to make it.

In general, evergreen hedges should be clipped as necessary through-out the summer, with any major reduction made in May, giving the hedge a long growing season to recover.

What Shape Top?
A strong, close-growing hedge such as box or *Cupressus* can be clipped flat on top. A rounded top is rather easier to manage. A few lovers of the highly formal garden prefer to angle the tops of their hedges to a ridge in the centre, like the gable of a house.

Which Hedge?
Hedges fall into three main classes. Those fit to put on a fine show to the world. Others, less expensive and imposing which will nevertheless make a firm "keep out" statement round a boundary. Then come those other, gentler, often flowering, scented and delightful hedges to use within the garden itself.

Fine Hedges

Yew: For a noble hedge there is no plant as good as the yew *(Taxus)*. Buy yew hedging from a good nursery and perhaps get their co-operation in planting it.

Once hedging plants arrive they should be put into the ground as soon as possible. Establish a yew hedge in spring or autumn. Plant 45 cm. apart for trees 60 cm. high; 60 cm. apart for trees one metre high, and one metre apart for those of one to one and a half metres.

Clip in early summer, about May, and again in August while the plants are young. Then later, once a year only, in August or early September.

Yew is slow-growing. It may be as long as 10 years before the hedge reaches its full dignity — but the result is worthwhile. Bear in mind that yew leaves are poisonous to horses and cattle.

Cypress or *Cupressus*: Another fine hedging plant. You can choose *leylandii* with its good resistance to salt sea breezes, or *horizontalis* which is native to southern Europe and with its wide spread, quickly forms a thick hedge.

Plant the young bushes 60 cm. apart and they should combine into a hedge in three years. Limit to a growth of 30 cm. a year, and trim the sides lightly in early spring and early autumn to encourage good growth low down.

Useful Everyday Hedges

Myporum, with its glossy green, year-round leaves makes a popular hedge which is satisfactory if kept well clipped. It is particularly effective when used on a street boundary marked by iron railings. The extra support counteracts its tendency to straggle. Myporum has the added advantage of growing quickly and so will soon provide protection for a new house.

Pittosporum: Many varieties of this shrub make good hedges. *P. tobira* from Japan with its sweetly-scented, creamy flowers makes an excellent screen and is particularly good by the sea. Prune in spring when necessary. Once established, it will often seed itself freely. *P. tenuifolium* has smaller leaves with wavy edges which sprout from dark shoots, and bears dark maroon flowers. Pittosporums are drought-resistant but appreciate water in hot weather.

Lantana: the variety *L. camera* will grow to a flowering and satisfactory hedge if kept well clipped. Give it water in summer and it will reward you with its flowers all the year round.

Firethorne — *Pyracantha* — from southern Europe, does particularly well on limestone soil, although it is not fussy and grows well anywhere in sun or part shade. The white flowers in early summer are followed by bright red berries. Remember that the roots are fragile, so buy container-grown plants. Clip the hedge occasionally in spring or summer and shorten out-of-place shoots after flowering.

Berberis, which is said to take its name from Barbary, gives us many types to choose from. One of the best is *B. stenophylla* which, when spaced 60 cm. apart, grows into an impenetrable hedge. Its long, prickly sprays bear sweetly-scented, yellow flowers. Trim immediately after flowering.

Two Country Hedges

To mark long boundaries in the country you can adopt the Spanish approach to hedges: plant a line of **bamboo** (good for cutting down when you need garden stakes).

Prickly Pear is another cheap plant which grows into a formidable boundary marker. The juicy fruit is edible.

Hedges Within the Garden

Inside the garden itself, lower flowering or herbal hedges can border a path, mark out some special feature such as a water garden, or merely give a sense of order by signalling the transition from one section of the garden to another.

Herbal Hedges

Bay: the culinary *Laurus nobilis* — not to be confused with the common laurel — can be clipped into hedges and screens, and its dark green, aromatic leaves picked for kitchen use. Plant 30 cm. apart.

Rosemary is a native of the Mediterranean. It makes an attractive low hedge with its narrow, aromatic leaves and will stand up to sun and dry conditions. The light blue flowers appear in early spring. Plant 30 cm. apart and pinch tips when young to make it branch out. Clip or shear older hedges only lightly.

Lavender makes a grey-green, aromatic low hedge producing the famous blue scented flowers. Plant in full sun 25 cm. apart. Prune immediately after flowering to keep the hedge shapely. To harvest lavender, cut the flower clusters as soon as they open, and dry in a cool place.

Other Attractive Hedges to Use Inside the Garden

Bottle-Brush — Callistemon. The favourite variety *Callistemon citrinus,* the Lemon bottle-brush, makes an unusual hedge, with its eye-catching red blooms made up of long, bristle-like stamens. Left alone it will make a tall shrub, but will withstand cutting into a hedge. Plant at 60 cm. apart.

Box comes in several varieties. The Japanese box is one of the most useful as it can be kept down to 15 cm. for small edgings or allowed to grow to a medium-sized, clipped hedge of one metre or more.

When making box edging, plant small divisions with roots attached in a shallow trench 15 cm. deep, nearly touching each other, and then earth up firmly leaving about 5 cm. above soil level. For a larger hedge plant 30 cm. high, about 30 cm. apart.

Hebe: All varieties are native of New Zealand. The boxleaf hebe, *Hebe buxifolia,* is smothered in white flowers and makes a low-growing hedge which is very little trouble to look after. It must not be sheared but can easily be shaped with secateurs.

Rose Hedges

Many varieties of bush roses make beautiful hedges and screens within the garden. Those with the right branching habit are specifically mentioned in many specialist rose catalogues. If you buy from a nursery, your rose grower will be able to suggest suitable bushes. Many would make a boundary hedge. However the blooms are so attractive that passers-by might not be able to resist the temptation of "just one rose", until your hedge is seriously depleted.

Roses for hedging are usually placed a little closer together than you would plant the same rose for display in a bed. They are not sheared, but shaped by cutting the individual shoots with secateurs.

Here is a selection of roses which have proved themselves in the making of beautiful hedges.

Rosa Mundi alias *Gallica versicolor.* This beautiful, open, pink-red splashed and striped rose can be dated back in Europe to the 17th century, and probably existed earlier. As well as making a garden display it is also good for cutting. It will grow about one metre high. Plant 75 cm. apart.

Marguerite Hilling: Pink and bushy. A strong grower to about two metres. Plant 125 cm. apart.

Mountbatten: A mimosa-yellow rose with large, double, scented blooms. The shining, green leaves clothe the bush at all levels. A beautiful rose. Plant 60 cm. apart.

Red Blanket: A red rose from Holland producing semi-double flowers all over the plant. A strong, sideways grower it makes a good, low hedge about 75 cm. high. Plant 70 cm. apart.

Rosy Cushion: A pink rose with an ivory heart, with a habit of growth very like Red Blanket. If you wish to mix a hedge of red and pink, grow them together in patches of colour. Plant 70 cm. apart.

Rosa Rugosa: In America sometimes known as the Sea Tomato. Originally a wild rose from North-East Asia, all varieties are extremely resistant to difficulties of climate, withstanding wind, drought and sea-spray. The prickly stems bear flowers 7-10 cm. across, all very fragrant, both single and double, and in colours ranging from pure white through cream to pink and a purplish-red. All bear round red hips like small tomatoes. Height varies according to variety from one to two and a half metres.

Zepherine Drouhin: The Rose Without a Thorn. An old rose from France, very free-flowering with its rich, pink colour and romantic perfume. Prune to make a hedge about two metres or a little less.

Other Hedges

Spiraea. There are many types, but the variety *Spiraea Vanhouttei* is the one to choose for an informal hedge. It grows quickly and easily to a height of almost two metres, with graceful, arching branches foamed with white blossom in midsummer. Prune for shape in late winter or very early spring. Plant at 60 cm.

Teucrium alias Germander. An evergreen little shrub with blue flowers which will stand up to sun and some drought. It will make a low, clipped hedge which should be sheared once or twice a year to encourage side branching. Plant about 30 cm. apart.

Wind-Breaks

Wind-breaks are a blessing to an exposed garden. The two points to remember are, that any shelter is better than none, and that for really effective protection you need defence in depth. For outer defences, hedges and bushes are better than trees as they are less likely to keel over in the wind. A hedge of bamboo, for instance, backed up by clumps of myporum and pittosporum can be prettied up with specimens of the tree mallow, Lavatera. Search for the variety *assugentiflora,* which is wind-resistant and will stand up to salt spray. It has leaves like a maple and bears pinkish and white striped flowers almost throughout the year. A fast grower, shear to keep it dense and wind-proof.

The orange Cape Honeysuckle, *Tecomaria,* left alone is a scrambler, but with hard pruning it will make a shrub of about two metres.

The oleander with its many varieties and colours of beautiful flowers can play its part in a combined wind-break operation, lending grace and gaiety to a utilitarian whole.

Perhaps the most useful single plant for protection from wind is the pampas-grass, *Cortaderia.* Coming from New Zealand and Argentina it will quickly form a dense, round clump impenetrable by wind. At the end of summer it produces tall, elegant plumes of cream or dusty pink which will, when necessary, sway with the wind but never break. For elegant clumps, cut down to the ground in winter.

Plant a Water Garden

ATER gardens are one of the pleasures of southern Spain, as was well understood by the Arabs, those great connoisseurs of earthly delights. The sheltered peace of the water gardens of the Alcázar in Seville show the charm that water can add to a garden.

Not only does a sheet of water bring a sense of relief on hot summer days; water is the natural home of some of the world's most beautiful plants.

Making a Water Garden

Pools for planting can be made in three ways, of varying cost and permanence.

The Plastic Sheet Pool

This is the cheapest and least durable method of making a pond.

1. Excavate the land to the shape and size required.
2. See that there are no sharp stones on the bottom that might puncture the skin (a layer of sand helps here).
3. Spread special plastic sheeting over the entire area of the pond.
4. Anchor it at the sides with a surround of paving stones.
5. Fill the pool up to the brim with water. It is important that the water reaches up to the pavers and that the pool is kept filled to the brim, otherwise sunlight will destroy the plastic film. In all subsequent gardening operations take great care never to puncture the plastic.

Made and treated with care, the plastic-lined pool will serve well.

The Fibreglass Pool

Attractive pool liners are available ready-formed in fibreglass in various shapes and depths. Excavate a hole of roughly the same shape and size as the shell. Put in the pool liner, and fill any gaps at the bottom or sides with soil or sand. It is important that the fibreglass is well supported, as otherwise it may crack under the weight of water.

A fibreglass shell can make an attractive water garden, especially when the size required is not too large.

The Cement-Lined Pool

This is for the gardener who wants a permanent feature.

You can consult a firm of gardening experts and let them undertake the work for you. They will discuss your particular site and the shape of the pool — whether circular, rectangular or irregular. They can supply an infrastructure of pipes, pumps and outlets, and can give you the variations of water depth which will allow you to supply the needs of different plants.

Or you can do the work yourself. In this case remember when you excavate the site to allow for a 15-cm. layer of waterproof cement. Many preparations are available. Consult your supplier and follow instructions carefully.

If possible, do all the work at the same time, as there can be a danger of "leak spots" if the work is done by stages, where one sheet of concrete joins another.

If it isn't possible to finish the work on one occasion, let the first lot of concrete dry out before adding to it. In addition, on starting work again, wet the edge of the existing concrete thoroughly. This will help the new concrete make a better join.

Make sure that the concrete dries slowly. Achieve this by covering the work with damp sacks and leaving them in place for 10 days. See that the sacks are always damp. In warm weather you may have to wet them two or three times a day. For a larger pool, reinforce the concrete with metal rods or wire netting, hiding the metal completely in the mix. Finish with a coating of special paint to prevent the concrete poisoning the water.

Siting the Pool

Set the pool in full sunshine, sheltered from the wind, and see that no leaf-shedding trees overhang, or are near it. If possible site it close to some lower ground, so that an outlet pipe with a stopcock can be built in to empty the pool if required. Failing this, dig a sump a cubic metre in volume, wall it with brick and fill with cinders, finished with a layer of soil topped by a loose paver.

You can help drainage by sloping the floor of the pool 10-15 cm. from one end to the other.

How Deep?

Depending on the plants you wish to grow, pools should be 45-75 cm.

deep. In a deeper pool, plants which love shallow water can be put in pots standing on bricks, placed in raised underwater beds, or on ledges built round the pool 25-30 cm. below the final surface of the water.

At the bottom of the pond lay a layer of good, rich soil at least 10 cm. deep. See that it contains plenty of manure.

When the pool has been filled, leave the water for a few days to mature. It will then lose any added chemicals, such as chlorine.

For a time the water will grow cloudy owing to the presence of algae (minute forms of life) which will later disappear of their own accord, when the pool is fully established.

Next, plant the oxygenating plants, sometimes known as oxygenating grasses. These are the vital underwater plants which do the work of keeping your pool clean and healthy. They absorb carbon dioxide from fish waste and decaying vegetation. In its place they give back oxygen which makes it possible for fish to survive. They give them a place to lay their eggs and by their presence control the ecological balance of the pool.

Allow two or three oxygenators for every square metre of water surface. If they grow too large they can be pruned away later. Plant in plastic containers and lower carefully into the water, or weigh down with stones and drop into the bottom soil.

It is possible to buy these little plants in "collections" from specialist dealers who can supply what is necessary according to the size of the pool. They are often available from aquarium shops and sometimes from the generous owners of existing pools.

The include: *anacharis* (sometimes known as *elodea), vallisneria, cabomba,* and miniature *sagitarria.*

Plants for the Water Garden

Many aquatic plants produce beautiful flowers and, for the sake of the fish who must also inhabit the pool to keep down mosquitoes, should cover nearly three-quarters of the surface. When the pool is planted, allow six weeks for the plants to get established before putting in fish and water snails. As a rule-of-thumb, allow two fish about 10 cm. long and a dozen water snails to every square metre of surface area.

The competition from fish, snails and water plants for the light and oxygen available will gradually bring about a natural balance, and you will have a pool of clean water which will not have to be changed in the foreseeable future.

A Choice of Water Flowers and How to Plant Them

Plant water flowers in plastic containers filled with good soil so that the leaves float on the surface. The soil should be covered with 10-15 cm. of water in most cases.

A sprinkling of pebbles on the surface of the pot will help keep the soil in position.

Floating Aquatics are laid gently on the surface of the water. They tend to increase rapidly and in winter should be pruned hard, so that the surface of the pond is not covered on more than one-fifth of its total area.

They include: fairy moss *(Azolla)* with its delicate fern-like foliage; the water hyacinth *(Eichhornia)* with its pale blue flowers borne on spikes; the water snowflake *(Nymphoides)* and the yellow water poppy *(Hydrocleys).*

Shallow Water Plants. Many plants grow in shallow water: the Sweet Flag *(Acorus),* whose aromatic roots and leaves contain an oil used in perfumes; the bog arum which lifts its furled, white flowers like little Easter lilies; the pink-flowering rush, and the aquatic iris (choose the variety *laevigata* and plant it in 5-10 cm. of water).

Water-Lilies. For most people, the pride of place in the pool is given to the water-lily. These beautiful flowers come from nearly every country in the world with the notable exception of New Zealand. They occur in a wide variety of colours, from gleaming white and delicate pink to carmine, copper and deep blue.

Some are tiny with miniature flowers scarcely 3 cm. across, while others bear huge blooms 30 cm. in diameter. Some flower by day, others by night. Some are fragrant, others scentless.

The method of planting all types varies very little. Take rich, firm, very moist, clayey soil, and plant the lily firmly in a basket or open-work plastic container lined with sacking to retain the soil.

In the case of those types grown from rhizomes, embed them horizontally, leaving just a little showing above the soil. Then lower the container below the surface of the water, supporting it on bricks to give a depth of 15 cm. for several weeks until the new growth is well established. Finally, remove the bricks one at a time until the container is standing on the bottom of the pond. If the plant is submerged away from the sun too quickly it might rot before it has time to become established.

Most water-lilies are not over-critical as to exact depth, but do better if kept somewhere near the conditions they prefer.

If yours come from a friend, take note how they were grown originally. If you buy from a specialist, he will advise as to depth.

A pool stocked with a variety of water-lilies springs into flower in April or May. The deep violet Stellata, flowers in June and continues far into the autumn. It is one of the few water-lilies to grow from a bulb not a rhizome.

Below is a list of some interesting varieties. Depths refer to depth of water *over* the plant.

Deep Pools (Depth 60-75 cm.)

Albatross: white.

Attraction: large, carmine flowers maturing to garnet red.

Escarboucle: large, deep dark red; an exceptionally lovely flower.

Gladstoniana: very large white with golden stamens.

Marliacea albida: white, fragrant and very free-flowering.

Marliacea rosea: fine shape, rose pink, paler towards the centre.

Picciola: large, crimson.

Tuberosa rosea: North American, scented, soft pink and a strong grower.

Medium Pools (Depth 30-50 cm.)

Braklei rosea: a very fine, fragrant rose pink.

Conqueror: red, flecked white.

Gloriosa: a large, red water-lily, very free-growing.

Indiana: orange-red, deepening with age to copper red, spotted foliage.

James Brydon: one of the best, deep carmine flowers sitting flat on the water.

Masaniello: globe-shaped deep pink, scented.

Rose Nymph: deep rose, scented.

Sunrise: very yellow with mottled leaves.

Shallow Pools (Depth 20-30 cm.)

Caroliniana: a pretty pink, scented.

Comanche: an apricot pink growing darker with age.

Paul Hariot: a widely-open flower of apricot, deepening to orange and orange-red.

Very small pools (need to be covered by about 15 cm. of water only)

Froebeli: will grow in patio pools and even in containers; white and pink varieties.

Pygmaea alba: white with deep green leaves.

Pygmaea helvolva: with soft yellow flowers and mottled foliage. One of the best of the miniature water-lilies.

Pygmaea rubis: red.

All water-lilies prefer still or only very slightly moving water. Remember also that they breathe from the top so will drown if constantly soaked by a splashing fountain.

Lotus. Plant as for a large water-lily in a pool 75-90 cm. deep in a really sheltered position. This is essential. These fabled flowers come from the Far East and will not tolerate wind or cold at any time. When in bloom they raise magnificent rose blossoms high above their large leaves.

Some gardeners succeed with this exotic flower by draining the pool in late autumn and covering the plants with a mixture of peat and manure until the following spring.

Water-Lilies are essential in any water garden. (Photo by AGE)

Oleander, a native to Spain, can be trained as a bush or a tree, serves as a wind-break or hedge, and is adapted to dry climates. (Photo by J. D. D.)

Climbing Bougainvillaea and Roses form a colourful archway.
(Photo by J. D. D.)

Two climbers perfectly adapted to a garden in Spain: Honeysuckle (above) and Jasmine (right). (Photo by AGE)

Climbing Plants

CLIMBERS are one of the pleasures of a Spanish garden. Brilliant and showy or green and cool, they add a new dimension by extending colour and scent from ground level high into the air. Although these plants are often natives of other parts of the world they flourish in the Spanish climate.

Exotic-looking climbers can also be practical. You can clothe the bare walls of a house with wistaria or bougainvillaea; cover an eyesore with jasmine; add privacy to a small garden with a floral trellis, or make a cool summer arbour.

A deciduous climber which gives shade in summer but lets in winter sunshine is a good choice close to the house. You can have blossom as well — wistaria is a good choice here — or plant a grape-vine and enjoy the fruit.

Climbing plants fall into four main groups. Some, like ivy, support themselves by "suckers", which are aerial roots; others such as Morning Glory or the passion flower have tendrils which will circle round anything as they climb upwards.

Some plants twine round any convenient stems and will spread upwards and outwards. It is surprising how far wistaria will go.

Other plants have to be tied into place, such as bougainvillaea or the climbing rose. Help them with wires, pergolas or bands of cloth tied to nails driven into a wall. You can also train them over a natural support such as an old tree.

Rules for Success

Prepare the ground by thorough digging. A tall, strong-growing plant will spread its roots widely, so dig over a site of two square metres for each. Enrich the ground with weathered manure or compost.

Don't plant too closely. Many strong climbing plants last a lifetime, growing upwards and outwards they give a splendid display. But don't overcrowd them or plant too close to a window. Leave the soil-ball intact when planting evergreens, and water carefully, especially during the first year.

Site at least two and a half metres apart for vigorous varieties such as bougainvillaea, grape-vines and wistaria. For all climbing plants, if they are to grow against a wall, make the planting hole 30 cm. away from the masonry. The base of a wall is one of the driest places in the garden.

A Collection of Climbers

Bougainvillaea — introduced to Europe from Brazil by the French navigator Louis de Bougainville, it is one of the glories of the gardens of Mediterranean Spain.

It will only set seed in certain parts of the world, one of these being Kenya. Several notable gardeners have come to Spain from this area bringing with them brilliant, man-made crosses. Stunning pinks, moon-pale yellows, whites and many other colours are now available. All are propagated from cuttings.

When planting, take care not to disturb the delicate roots. Train bougainvillaea with a firm hand. Cut out any side-shoots and main stems which give too much bulk. Remove also any pale "water shoots" which occur. This fine, strong grower needs to be secured to a sturdy support. Don't over-feed or over-water.

Clematis — known as the queen of climbers — has been developed into a wide variety of beautiful colours and styles.

Give any clematis rich, well-drained soil, water liberally and remember the saying, "Clematis loves its feet in the shade and its face in the sun." Don't, however, allow it to be touched by hot, midday sun.

Regular pruning isn't essential, but varieties that flower in spring and early summer may be thinned or shortened when the flowers fade. Cut back summer and autumn flowering kinds in winter as needed. Mulch the plants liberally every spring with rich compost or old manure, and support as necessary.

Cape Honeysuckle — Tecomaria — is a tough, long-lasting plant which scrambles through bushes and into trees, and will continue to produce its orange flowers even if neglected. It is at its best as part of an informal, mixed planting and contrasts well with the blue flowers of plumbago.

Cobaea — a fast-growing annual which supports itself by tendrils. The large flowers, which are rather like Canterbury bells, open pale and darken to purple. Grow from seed.

Grape-Vine — decorative, fruitful and useful (for shade, and scented barbecue fuel as well as fruit), the vine needs a sunny, airy position. Buy from the nursery a climbing vine.

Fill an ample planting hole with a mixture of peat and old manure. Water your vine well in spring and summer, but very little at other times. Nourish with a weak liquid fertilizer once a month during the growing season. Prune in autumn after leaf-fall.

If you want the shade of an arbour, prune lightly, cutting off only those shoots which hang down from the support.

For more fruit, cut out spindly or overcrowded canes and leave strong side-shoots 15-25 cm. apart, cutting them back to the second bud.

Honeysuckle — one of the most sweetly-scented plants in the garden, honeysuckle will support itself on other plants. As far as possible choose a shaded position for the roots, it will make its own way up to the light.

Ivy — choose a delicate, small-leaved variety, either all green or variegated with cream. Looks dramatic against a white wall. Don't be afraid to keep in check by pruning drastically. It will soon grow again.

Jasmine — many varieties will climb, including the white, very fragrant "common jasmine" from Iran, Kashmir and China, and the quick-growing Spanish jasmine. Give normal soil, water and some support.

Morning Glory — Ipomoea. Both annual and perennial types grow easily and mix well together. Sow annual seed in spring, but after one sowing it will reseed itself for years appearing in unlikely but attractive places.

The perennial variety known as Moonflower opens at night into scented, pale flowers 15 cm. across. Soak the hard seed for one or two days and sow in spring or autumn.

Passion Flower — a vigorous climber producing beautiful flowers. The varieties *edulis* and *quadrangularis* give edible fruit as well. You can even grow it in a container. Give support and thin out well.

Plumbago — an attractive climber for a mixed planting where its pale blue flowers contrast well with dark blue morning glory or orange Cape honeysuckle. Once established, it needs little water or fertilizer.

Solandra — the Cup-of-Gold vine — a fast-growing climber which produces spectacular flowers of yellowish orange, which often smell of apricots. These natives of tropical America grow well in Spain. Support this rampant grower, and prune to encourage lateral shoots and more flowers, which appear in spring and intermittently at other times. In hot situations keep the roots cool. Solandra will stand up to wind and salt breezes.

Thunbergia — of the many varieties of thunbergia available perhaps the most beautiful is the blue thunbergia *grandiflora,* sometimes known as the Sky Flower. Train it over an arch or pergola as the clusters of dramatic flowers hang downwards. Remove spent blossom and you will have a long flowering season. Buy plants or grow from seed planted in spring. Other varieties produce orange or dark blue flowers. Water well in hot weather.

Wistaria — as this climber lives long, grows tall and produces at best a mass of lovely flowers, it is worth buying a good plant to begin with. You may wish to buy more than one, of differing colours, such as the normally grown purple, the more delicate white, deep purple or pink.

Special soil is not important; water is valuable and support essential. Train over a firm support as the weight of the plant will eventually become considerable.

The main flush of flowers comes in spring on bare branches; later flowers peep out from among leaves.

Wistaria will twine its way up a strong cord or festoon an old tree. Prune only as necessary to achieve the effect you want.

A walkway shaded by wistaria, with bunches of purple and white flowers hanging downwards, is a sight to remember.

House-Plants

MY Spanish friend arrived with a present — an attractive basket of potted plants.

"Put them in the light, out of the draught and line the basket with plastic," she said as she handed them over. A scientist by profession, trained in lucid thought, her instructions were apt and accurate.

The plants had come from a good florist and were well potted and properly grown. Eight months later they were still in excellent order, having never spent a day out of the living-room.

This is the sort of result we all want to see from our potted plants, and in the case of larger specimen plants, the healthy life-span is measured not in months but in years.

Care of House-Plants

To keep pot plants growing well over a long period is a skill easily acquired.

Normally, house plants need a good light just short of full sunshine, and dislike draughts. A professional exhibitor at the Chelsea Flower Show in London told me that smaller plants do better when grouped together, and that the pots should be allowed to dry out between each watering. A quick touch of your finger among the leaves will tell you whether the compost is moist or dry.

Don't allow them to stand in saucers of water for more than half an hour as waterlogged soil prevents the roots from breathing and the plants will not thrive. When watering time comes, water thoroughly so that the moisture will reach the entire root system.

For this reason I like to water room plants in the kitchen in the evening. Stand them in water for half an hour. At the same time water the plants from above. Spray or sprinkle the leaves and flowers and then leave to drain overnight. In the morning they will look as fresh as the day they were bought. There are of course exceptions. Large plants cannot be moved about and must be watered where they stand.

Cacti and succulents need full sunshine and much less water, while African violets like to suck up their water from below, with just a light spray or sprinkling over the leaves. (They love moist heat, coming as they do from the steamy equatorial jungle. Nothing does a tired African violet more good than a few days in a light bathroom, out of direct sunlight.)

Food for room plants must be given with care. Not that they don't like it, but given too much they may well grow beyond the allotted space. Feed with liquid fertilizer once a month during the growing period, or insert sticks of slow-release fertilizer into the pots. I have found Jobe's Plant Food Spikes successful and labour saving. Made in America, they are now widely distributed. Each application lasts for about 60 days and cannot overfeed or underfeed your plant. As with all manufactured fertilizers, follow the maker's instructions.

Feed African violets with weak liquid fertilizer in the water in the bottom of the pot. Don't apply until the first buds are showing and continue during the flowering season. Fertilizer given when there is no bloom results in too many leaves growing, at the expense of flowers.

Pots and Potting Mixtures

Plastic pots retain moisture for about three times as long as earthenware pots and so save work. Some people prefer the look of earthenware pots, and as they weigh more, they are more stable and suitable for a large plant.

In every case see that containers have good holes in the bottom, covered with small, broken pieces of pot. The drainage must be excellent.

Buy special potting soil either from a nursery gardener or garden centre. You need to provide a light, open mixture which will hold moisture far longer than ordinary soil. Packs of many named brands are available including "soilless" composts, based on peat, sand and fertilizers. These are an indoor gardener's dream providing an ideal growing medium. They contain enough fertilizer to last three months, after which you will have to feed your plants normally.

A Choice of Plants

It is almost impossible to single out a choice of plants from the many varieties available, but try the following for hardiness, appearance, long life, or for all three qualities.

Noble Plants

Aspidistra — a heavy-duty plant from China that will fill a difficult corner where light and temperature are not ideal, and yet will live for years. Consider the green or the variegated varieties. Both appreciate an occasional wiping with a weak solution of milk and water, or water alone.

Monstera — a fine plant for a large space, with dramatic, deeply cut leaves. Not too demanding as to light. Looks well grown with a philoden-dron.

Palm — The Canary Island palm makes a fine indoor specimen for many years when given a light place to grow.

Change the upper part of the soil of all large pot plants early each spring.

Specimen Plants to Use in Groups or Alone

These plants will grow together under similar conditions, or make interesting specimens on their own.

Aluminium Plant — Pilea — gets its name from its dark green leaves which are streaked with silver-grey.

Begonia Rex — a strong plant with many different leaf variations. The branches are brittle but a damaged plant will soon sprout again.

Cyperus — the Umbrella Plant — makes a decorative pot plant, holding its green leaves, like the ribs of an umbrella, on long, slender stems. It is not fussy about soil but must have plenty of water.

Dumb Cane — Dieffenbachia — (anyone unwise enough to suck the stem is afflicted with a swollen mouth which makes him speechless) has variegated leaves and forms a valuable addition to an ornamental group.

Elephant's Ears will slowly grow into a fine plant with large, heart-shaped leaves of medium green. As old leaves die, cut them off and a trunk will become established. New plants will form beside the old, making an attractive group. A tender plant which won't withstand wind. If "tears" form on the tips of leaves, the plant has been overwatered. Turn pot occasionally to maintain shapely growth.

Mother-in-Law's Tongue — Sansevieria — gets its English name from its sharp, pointed leaves. A tough, good-looking plant growing narrowly upwards, it will withstand difficult conditions, preferring only not to be moved about too much. The leaves of mottled green are edged with bands of green or yellow.

Peperomia — an attractive, low plant with heart-shaped leaves, useful for the front of a group.

Spider Plant — Chlorophytum — an attractive plant producing a crown of narrow, green leaves with a white central stripe, which will withstand neglect (but is of course better without it). Runners emerge bearing white flowers which later form new plants on the end of arching stems. An excellent plant to put on a high shelf or in a hanging basket to display the cascading, downward growth.

For Colour

Busy Lizzie — Grow in a cool place, giving plenty of water. Many brilliant colours and variations have been developed in recent years.

Christmas Cactus — a leaf-flowering cactus which is covered with blooms, often rosy pink, around Christmas time. Keep outside in a sheltered, shady place during the summer, and bring in to a light but not sunny place in October. Don't move from the chosen place. Sudden change may result in the dropping of buds.

Neoregelia — a tender plant forming rosettes of stiff, green leaves round a central cup. The cup and the leaves around it are coloured brilliant red. Nurture this expensive and exotic house-plant with the best place you can find — warm, bright (no direct sun) and draught-free. Fill the central cup with water, preferably with bottled drinking water, and keep it filled.

Poinsettia — a favourite plant to give as a Christmas gift as the brilliant red "flowers" appear at Christmas time. The apparent petals are in fact bracts and the true flowers are the small yellow centres. After flowering, either throw away, plant in the garden, or try for flowers another year. Gradually dry off after blooming and cut back hard in April, beginning again the watering cycle.

Clinic for Sick House-Plants

Sometimes, especially at the end of winter and after some years' service, house-plants appear dull and lifeless. They probably have outgrown their containers.

Tip the plant out of its pot. If roots are evident filling the soil and circling round, take the following steps: for a plant with a single crown, like a spider plant, crumble the soil and prune away thick, solid roots. Leave only a network of fine feeding roots. Repot in light, fluffy soil.

For a plant with many stems, such as an aspidistra, cut the root-ball into sections, making sure that each section contains both roots and leaves. Repot as before, and your plants will be rejuvenated.

The Fascination of Ferns

ERNS in their many and beautiful forms are proving that they display well and last long in modern homes in Spain, whether sited in the house, on the patio or planted out in the open garden. Yet to do so they need the right living conditions, and to find out what these are, it is helpful to look back on their long history.

Ferns are an extremely ancient form of plant life. They appeared awesomely early, somewhere after the emergence of land and before the arrival of animal life.

For this reason, even the ferns we know today have their own prehistoric forms of provision for the propagation of their species. They normally produce no flowers, for what was the point of the attraction of colour and scent in a world where there were no insects? They produce no fruit, for there were no birds to eat it and spread the seeds.

Strictly speaking, ferns do not produce seed, for a seed is a complete entity, a plant pack in miniature which needs only moisture and favourable conditions to grow into a new plant. Ferns produce spores which must fall on to a damp surface for the actual mating of the male and female organisms to take place. The male swims on a light film of moisture to the female "egg" which, once fertilized, swells and produces a green, filmy organism. From this the new ferns are born.

The ferns we grow are sterile. The ferns we can raise from them are also sterile. Sexual activity only takes place in alternate generations, in the green film on the soil. From their early history we learn that water is one of the essential elements in a fern's life.

Ferns to Grow and How to Grow Them

Ferns green and cool, ferns delicate or sturdy, ferns with strange forms, and ferns like trees, are all suitable for growing in Spain. Go to a nursery or garden shop and ask for an *helecho,* fern, and they will almost certainly be able to show you a selection. Good ferns are often available in markets and supermarkets. A collection of ferns is easy to start and interesting to build up. You can even grow many lovely species from spores.

Although there are many thousands of different ferns in the world with slightly varying needs, most ferns prefer a shaded, draught-free situation, indoors or out, with open, peaty soil and plenty of water.

Many grow excellently in pots or planters, but unlike other container-grown plants, they should not be given artificial fertilizers. If so treated, they tend to respond over-exuberantly and then die. Use only a top dressing of fresh soil or a little bone-meal or other organic fertilizer in spring and autumn.

In their ancient habitat, ferns grew on the ground or in soil lodged in the branches of trees. They were not parasites feeding on the host plant but, like orchids or African violets, merely lived in pockets of soil which had built up from decaying vegetation caught in crevices of trees. For this reason many ferns do exceptionally well in hanging baskets or in pots set high, where the fronds can grow upwards and cascade down towards the ground.

Group delicate ferns together. They form their own mini-climate and so thrive better. Or stand pots on pebbles in a dish with water at the bottom. The humidity of the atmosphere will be higher.

A Selection of Ferns

Boston Fern *(Nephrolepis)* — this might be called Spain's favourite house fern on account of its long, graceful, deeply-cut fronds which arch out from the centre of the plant.

Give it the normal fern treatment of moist, peaty soil; keep it well away from sunlight, draughts and sources of heat; water regularly and the Boston fern will grace your home for years. Because of its strong, arching growth, it looks particularly well in a pedestal container, or displayed in a hanging basket.

Brake *(Epteride)* — an attractive, small fern native to Spain and the Mediterranean region. The undivided, faintly crinkled, glossy green leaves are narrow and ribbon-like, making a good pot plant for the house or patio. A moisture lover, the *epteride* enjoys a shadowy situation, moist soil and misting of the fronds in warm weather.

Maidenhair Fern — grows wild in several parts of Spain and has been found not far from Marbella on the Costa del Sol.

This fern appears particularly delicate, as each spur is made up of a host of small, kidney-shaped fronds, each lightly joined to the central mid-rib by a fine stem — a beautiful fern which does well in the house.

Staghorn Fern — one of the most dramatic ferns available in Spain. Far from being delicate, the fertile fronds are long and fleshy, rich green and branching like the horns of a stag. A fern which originally made its home high in the branches of trees, it makes a dramatic decoration for a shaded patio, cascading downwards one metre or more.

It is ideally grown in live sphagnum moss wired on to a log or a piece of cork, and is often offered for sale in this way. It can also be grown in a peaty compost in a pot or hanging basket.

Water freely in spring and summer, being careful — in the case of a log-based fern — not to dislodge the compost. In winter, water only when the surface of the compost is just dry to the touch.

An expert's tip is to tuck an old banana skin into the limited compost. The fern will appreciate the extra source of nitrogen.

Some gardeners attach a staghorn fern to a living tree. First choose a tree which doesn't shed its bark. Then drive nails straight into the wood and attach with galvanized wire the fern with its pack of moss. Don't wire round a branch or trunk, as in time the tree will grow and the wire will cut into the vital cambium layer lying just below the bark.

Eventually the staghorn will completely cover its supports, and become a most attractive and dramatic feature.

Fern Look-alikes

A few plants look like ferns, behave like ferns, but strictly speaking do not belong to the fern family.

Asparagus Fern — from South Africa, this is the delicate, fern-like plant much used by florists. It grows well in a shaded part of the garden or patio. Train it carefully and it will climb for three metres or more, and looks particularly attractive displaying its ethereal fronds against a white wall. But the asparagus fern is deceptively tough. Even in an abandoned garden it will endure for years. Give it the care of shade, water and reasonably good garden soil, and it will become a lovely feature, whether grown in a garden bed or patio planter.

Smilax — a bolder variety of the same plant with needles rather than fronds. It makes a handsome wall plant and will grow to five metres, bearing small, white flowers followed by decorative berries.

As both the above are members of the lily family and not true ferns, they benefit from an occasional application of a complete fertilizer.

Selaginella — a small, fern-like plant that loves moisture and will put up with a high degree of shade. On its own it makes a pretty little pot plant, and is particularly useful in hanging baskets as surface cover for high, arching ferns, quickly covering bare stems and the basket itself with a delicate cloud of green fronds.

Ferns Without a Common Spanish Name

Many ferns grow well in Spain passing under the casual family name *"helecho"* (fern).

Bird's Nest Fern (offered in one Spanish mail-order catalogue under its Latin name *Asplenium nidus-avis,* and very widely available elsewhere) is one of the few ferns whose leaves are entire, as opposed to being cut into leaflets.

This good-looking fern with its big, mid-green leaves is particularly suitable for pot culture as it originally grew in pockets of soil on trees, and so has a root system which is small in relation to the rest of the plant.

Give it a light, well-drained potting mixture in keeping with its original habitat. When grown in the garden, supply plenty of humus — peat or well-rotted compost — so that the delicate roots can penetrate easily.

Ostrich Plume Fern and **Shuttlecock Fern** — both natives of Europe and North Africa — have the habit of sending up growth in the shape of one or several shuttlecocks.

The origin of this shape is at the same time sophisticated and simple. In the crowded vegetation of the primordial forests where ferns had their beginnings, nourishment had to be competed for. The Shuttlecock family decided not to rely on their root-systems alone. Their "shuttlecock" formation collected falling leaves from trees above and converted them into plant food. In other words, they made their own compost.

Unfurling fronds of the Ostrich Plume, known in America as "Fiddleheads", are edible and were served at one time at the Four Seasons restaurant in New York, listed as "Fiddlehead Ferns Gratinés". But for most of us these are ferns to look at rather than eat.

The shuttlecock fern in particular makes a dramatic pot plant, holding its green shuttlecocks half a metre into the air. Grow it as cool as possible and give plenty of moisture.

Some ferns have different names in English in different parts of the world. **Hard Ferns** (in the UK), **Rib Ferns** (in the USA) and **Water Ferns** (in Australia), are all names for the same family of ferns, *Blechnum*.

From this large family, *Gibbum* (40-100 cm. tall) develops a trunk and looks like a quick-growing cycad. Its deeply-cut fronds form a close circle on top of the stem. Give it a medium amount of light (naturally, no direct sunlight) and plenty of water. Groom it well as it grows and you will have a good-looking container plant.

Brazilian Fern grows about one metre high with wavy, green fronds which have a reddish tinge when young.

Hammock Fern — a smaller member of the same family, also with reddish new growth. Although like other ferns it should be kept moist, it can do with more light than most, and can — in an emergency — stand up to rather dryer conditions. It grows to a useful height of about 30 cm.

Tree Ferns — today's descendants of the great ferns which formed part of the world's vegetation millions of years ago. Large by our standards, modern tree ferns are lilliputian compared to their great ancestors, whose decayed vegetation helped to form the world's coal seams.

Tree ferns grow anything from 30 cm. to 12 metres or more. They carry their fronds high, forming a stem as each circle of leaves dies to be replaced by the new growth above it.

Interesting as pot and tub plants, many grow slowly and last for years before outgrowing their containers.

Give them the same care as other ferns, but be careful not to let water sink into the crowns, as it might cause the stem to rot. In hot weather, water the trunks as well as the roots and fronds.

If you can't buy a ready-grown tree fern, consider growing your own from spores.

How to Grow Ferns from Spores

Use a good proprietary, peat-based compost. It will already have been sterilized. Open a fresh bag — the moisture will be just right.

Use a clean pot, fill it with compost and firm the surface. Sow the fine, dust-like spores on the moist surface but don't cover with soil. Cover the pot at once with a sheet of clean glass and turn it every day.

Stand the pot in shade but not in darkness as the spores need light to germinate. Then stand the pot in a saucer of water. Professionals add a granule or two or permanganate of potash to this water to deter the growth of moulds.

Maintain a gentle heat of 20 °C and expect developments in anything from 5-15 days. Some varieties will appear quickly. Some may be much slower to germinate — anything up to six months, or even longer. When the first fronds appear, separate the little plants to prevent overcrowding.

Ferns can also be propagated by division when multiple crowns develop. Others, like the Mother fern, grow baby ferns on their leaves. Detach and plant them. (In nature the weight of the new plant eventually pulls the frond down until it touches the earth, when a new set of roots grows.)

Fern spores are on sale by post from Suttons Seeds and Thompson and Morgan (see page 189 for addresses).

*A Fern by the pool appreciates the humidity without dropping foliage
in the water. (Photo by J. D. D.)*

Covered terrace offers ideal home for both house-plants and outdoor plants.
(Photo by W. C.)

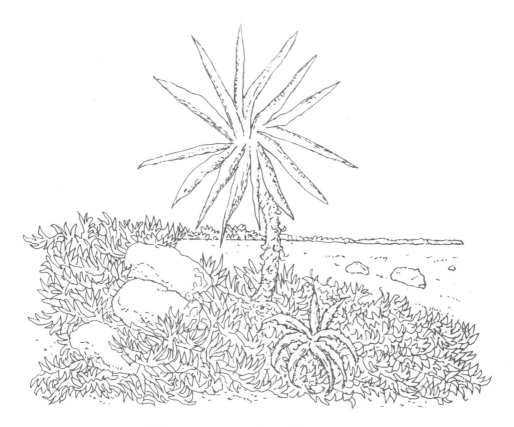

Ground Cover

ROUND cover plants can be of the greatest use in some gardens. In others they are not needed at all.

Their main uses are to stabilize banks by holding the soil together and so preventing erosion in rainy weather, or to cut down on work by covering some areas with plants which will look after themselves, clothe the ground attractively and, by their presence, suppress weeds.

Aloe — any of the many varieties of this spiny, "red-hot poker" look-alike — a perennial succulent — cover banks with fine, upstanding plants that add a bright touch of flame to the garden in winter. Plant them where you don't want to garden intensively and they will look after that particular part of your land for you, practically unaided.

The yellow-flowered variety, the Barbados aloe, has long been respected in its native habitat as a cure for all types of cuts, burns and inflammation. Today scientists report that this plant does indeed possess valuable healing qualities.

Some gardeners grow the Barbados aloe near the back door so that a cut leaf is quickly available to deal with any minor kitchen accident.

Gazania — the Treasure Flower from South Africa, doubles as a garden flower in its own right and as ground cover. Gazanias are low-growing perennials which love the sun and bear large, showy daisy flowers throughout the summer.

Plant the trailing variety for ground cover. It will spread quickly, filling spaces with brilliant yellow or orange flowers.

Ice-Plant — a low-growing, fleshy perennial succulent with bright, daisy-like flowers, much used for road-side plantings by municipal gardeners. The ice-plant will take full sun.

Set out young plants in autumn or grow from cuttings. Water when necessary to get established. Later, only very occasional watering is needed, just enough to keep the leaves plump and green.

Recently the ice-plants Lampranthus and Carpobrotus have been listed as separate subjects. The flower colour and size varies, but all are tough, brilliant and valuable allies for dealing with hot, dry places.

Periwinkle — a low, creeping plant with blue flowers, useful to cover less important parts of the garden. Give it some shade and occasional watering and it will last for years.

Rock-Rose — Cistus. One of Spain's wild flowers. Useful in larger gardens for covering dry, sunny banks and controlling erosion.

Pinch out the tops of young plants to make the growth more bushy and, when established, cut out old, woody stems occasionally. Once planted, little or no watering is needed. The brilliant flowers come early.

Rosemary — choose the dwarf rosemary which grows 30 cm. tall with a 1.5-2.5 metre spread. Its pale lavender flowers and fine, aromatic leaves make it a real asset as well as a labour-saving plant.

Violet — fill flower-beds on the shady side of the house or in the shadow of trees with massed violets. For much of the year the closely clustering leaves hide the soil and look pleasant. When in bloom, an air off the half-hidden flowers is a delight to remember.

Lawn substitutes such as creeping thyme, Pennyroyal, Corsican mint and camomile are also useful as ground cover. They look their best either planted in sweeps or in specifically defined areas of the garden.

Fruit in Your Garden

ANY types of fruit grow easily in Spanish gardens. For generations village homes and cottages out in the country have had a fruit tree or two tucked away behind the house. Custard apples, figs and pomegranates have supplemented the family diet at no cost.

Foreigners coming to live in Spain have brought with them new tastes and new varieties. Now a wide choice of delicious fruit is available to grow at home. Look round the nurseries or order what you need by post.

Avocado: Southern Spain is one of the few areas in Europe where soil, availability of water and climate favour this delicious fruit. Good nurseries sell stock from avocados imported officially from the USA. If you want year-round avocados consult your dealer, and arrange to plant varieties which fruit at different times of the year. Shelter from wind.

Left alone, the avocado will grow to a tall tree giving good shade. You can control its shape by pruning so that fruit is born on lateral branches which are easier to reach.

Avocados like water, but good drainage is essential. Make a wide watering basin, and only water enough to reach the top 60 cm. of soil, as the tree is a shallow rooter.

If your garden is small, buy a dwarf variety which can even be grown in a patio bed or in a container.

Fig: Fig trees are hardy and require little attention, often producing enough fruit when left alone. If you wish to increase the crop, prune to remove crowded branches and allow light and air to reach the centre of the tree.

Do not over-water when the figs are forming, or the tree may drop its crop prematurely. Over-watering when the fruit is almost ripe will produce figs which are too soft and lack flavour. A fig tree needs to grow hard. For the best-flavoured fruit, leave it alone.

Smaller varieties of figs will grow in a container and make decorative patio trees which bear fruit as well. Give a little more attention in these less-than-natural circumstances. Don't let the soil dry out in summer and feed from time to time, as the soil in a container soon becomes exhausted. Fertilize in early spring and again in summer if the fig appears to need it.

Custard Apple: An easy fruit to grow, plant the custard apple in average soil in a courtyard bed, or near a terrace where its intriguing scent fills the air. Water moderately. It also benefits greatly from spraying during the hot weather.

A young tree grows quickly for the first three or four years of its life, and then settles down to become eventually a tree about five metres high with a spread as wide, or even wider. Don't prune at all for the first five years, then cut out old wood each year after fruiting to encourage new fruit-bearing shoots. Prune as soon as the last fruit is picked.

The fleshy flowers start to form in spring and go on for three months, giving a correspondingly long fruiting period.

Guava: Completely foolproof, once established the guava bears loads of fruit. Give it good soil to start with, a little water occasionally, and you are assured of a good crop. It will grow from seed to a fruiting tree in nine or 10 years. Buy a good specimen and enjoy your guavas almost at once.

Apricot: Makes a good dual-purpose fruit and shade tree, very attractive when in fruit. Give a sheltered position, good soil and some water. Prune in summer to give circulation of air, and allow light to enter to the centre of the tree.

Plum: The plum tree prefers a rich, well-cultivated soil, and dislikes pruning. If essential to avoid overcrowding, prune carefully in summer after the fruit has been harvested.

Soft Fruit

Strawberry: The queen of soft fruits, strawberries are easy to grow in Spain and mature faster than in colder climates.

Start your preparations in October by allocating an area of good, rich soil. Not very much space is needed as the Spanish method is intensive.

Dig the soil into parallel ridges which run from north to south so that each plant will get its fair share of winter sunshine. Make the ridges 25 cm. high and 30 cm. wide at the base with a channel between each just wide enough to walk along for picking. Then enclose the whole bed with a retaining earth wall, so that when you irrigate the water will not escape.

Next, plant the runners, not on top of the ridge but on each side, east and west, just below the crown. Plant 45 cm. apart on both sides, and stagger them so that no two plants are opposite each other. In this way the ridge will support one plant about every 22 cm. of its length.

As a final economy of space, plant a lettuce seedling on top of the ridge between each plant. Plant a few at a time so that you get "on-flow" lettuces as well as "on-flow" strawberries.

The exact timing of the crop will vary a little depending on the region of Spain and the type of strawberry. On the Costa del Sol, Royal Sovereign planted on November 1st will yield the first picking about March 1st of the following year.

You may not need to water all the time. Adjust to the rainfall. When rain stops, or until it begins, water by hose-pipe three nights a week at sunset. Just flow the water into the channels between the ridges. Don't spray the plants directly; the roots will find their way down to the water.

For some time after planting, the strawberries will appear to be making no progress at all. Don't lose heart, for the root system is becoming established. This is the time to give the soil a light dusting of sulphate of ammonia, known locally as *sulfato,* but be careful not to let the powder touch the leaves.

No straw is needed in Spain and, surprisingly, no netting. Each plant develops a dense crown of leaves with the fruit well hidden and safe from birds.

Raspberry: Buy good canes and plant them between autumn and early spring in good soil in a *sol y sombra* (half-sun, half-shade) situation 30 cm. apart in rows spaced at least 2.5 metres apart. Beneath citrus trees often proves a suitable place.

Spread the roots out widely in a planting hole just deep enough to cover the upper roots with 5 cm. of soil. At the end of winter cut the canes down to 15 cm. In the spring new shoots will sprout up. Pick off any flowers the first year.

The secret of success is to surround raspberries with a 15-centimetre-deep mulch. Apply the mulch damp and keep it damp. This keeps the roots cool and prevents any evaporation. The ideal mulch is made of any good compost. As the canes grow, tie them to strong supports. They will bear next year's fruit.

You can save work by planting one of the newer varieties such as the Swiss Zeva, which bears fruit on the growth made each year. Prune all canes to within 15 cm. of the ground in January. They need no support.

Loganberry, Boysenberry and **Blackberry:** The loganberry was a chance cross-breeding between a blackberry and a raspberry, found in the garden of Judge Logan of Santa Cruz in 1881. The boysenberry originated in California in 1925, the result of a deliberate cross achieved by a Mr Boysen between a dewberry and loganberry. Both like the same growing conditions as raspberries, but are tougher and more prolific. Prune by cutting out old wood. Buy thornless varieties when possible.

Cultivated blackberries bear more luscious fruit than the wild bushes. Rampant growers, treat them as loganberries.

Melon: This fruit grows beautifully in Spanish gardens, but is a truly tropical plant, killed by even a light frost. In warm gardens plant seeds in March. Elsewhere plant two weeks after the last expected frost. Enthusiasts develop individual methods of growing this delicious fruit. One grows his on the side of his compost heap. Others grow on raised ridges in hollow, circular mounds. The aim is to supply plenty of water to the roots without wetting the plants themselves.

For the ridge method, make a long mound one metre wide and half a metre high, sowing seeds on the top, one metre apart. You can then irrigate at the bottom of the mound without water touching the fruit.

Other growers make a circular mound, one metre in diameter, with a depression in the middle, then plant the seeds in the centre, and train the shoots over the rim as they grow. They then irrigate the centre, so that the roots receive the water and the fruit outside remains dry. In a mound one metre in diameter plant six seeds 2 cm. deep in a 20-25 cm. circle. If they become overcrowded, remove the weakest.

Growing melons at home means that you can choose a variety with a size and flavour to suit your own particular needs and taste. A great favourite is Ogen, developed in Israel, which has a particularly fine scent and flavour, although many other strains can be grown. In the case of Ogen, each vine will produce up to 10 melons which mature in 70-73 days.

Make successional sowings of all varieties for an onflow supply. According to local conditions, you will get a superb crop from August to October. When supply exceeds demand, store the surplus in nets in a cool, sunless place. It will keep well into winter, often supplying excellent melons on Christmas day.

If space is limited, plant a bush melon. It takes only one square metre of land, matures early and produces a good crop. Minnesota Midget is one of the best, with 10-cm. orange-fleshed fruit so tender it can be eaten right down to the rind.

Currants: Whether red, black or white, currants grow in a shaded place where a little sunshine falls, either in early morning or late afternoon. Prune to keep a balance between first-, second- and third-year canes, as fruit is borne on each.

Monstera deliciosa: A widely-grown plant whose fruit is not often understood in Spain. Give this good-looking plant fertile soil, water and part-shade, and long fruits, shaped rather like cucumbers, will form among the deeply-cut leaves.

A lemon grower from Sicily reports that since he has planted a monstera under each lemon tree, he receives as much money from the exotic fruit on the ground as he does from the lemon crop above. The customers for the monsteras are gourmet restaurants in Rome. The taste is delicious but hard to describe, being somewhere between a banana and a pineapple.

Growing Vegetables

ECENTLY there has been a strong upsurge of interest in growing vegetables in one's own garden. This may seem strange in Spain, where every market has its rich harvest of brilliant vegetables. Yet even gardeners with a good supply at hand often prefer to grow some crops at home.

Some consider convenience. Who wants to make a journey to market just for a handful of fresh green herbs or a head of lettuce?

Then there is the question of special varieties: plum tomatoes perhaps (only available for a fairly short period, and most go for canning) — or real English parsley.

Another compelling reason is that many people like to know what they are eating: that it has been organically grown, is free from harmful pesticides and comes from the garden sparkling fresh with all vitamins intact.

Today it is widely understood that vitamin-rich fresh food contributes greatly to our health and well-being. A survey of schoolchildren showed that those from families who grew their own vegetables, and therefore could afford to serve two or three at a meal, freshly picked, had a better health record than children from families which relied on bought produce.

Finally, and this applies to all groups of kitchen-garden enthusiasts, whether of the organic or chemical fertilizer-cum-insecticide brigade, they grow vegetables for flavour and for fun. Where necessary many have worked out ingenious ways of doing so.

Planning a Kitchen Garden

Ideally, choose a bright, sheltered place with fertile soil. If your land is windy, plan shelter belts of walls or hedges. If the soil is poor, improve it by cultivation and the addition of peat, fertilizer, compost or farmyard manure. If the soil is beyond redemption, either buy more and spread it to a depth of 30 cm. on the existing land, or, more manageably, make raised beds — like giant planters on the ground, and so see that your crops get the soil they need. If you garden on a steep hillside, terrace the land to prevent erosion.

To grow vegetables well, soil should be fertile, well-drained, well-tilled, and free from weeds. Sunlight — an easy requirement — and water (sometimes more difficult) are also needed.

Start a compost heap, avoiding perennial weeds, tough stalks and any diseased material. Use an accelerator or rely on water alone to keep the heap moist and help make a rich humus.

Don't plant the same crop in the same place two years running. Brassicas for instance take nitrogen from the earth. Peas and beans add it. This need to rotate crops does not apply to the onion family, which can grow happily in the same place year after year, or to perennial vegetables such as asparagus or globe artichokes.

Assess your needs before you buy seeds or plants. How much does your family really need? Do you want mainly spring and autumn harvesting or are you prepared to grow year-round crops? Some gardeners living where water is in short supply — in Gibraltar for instance — start in spring when their water-catchment tanks are full; continue till summer when the supply runs out, and then rest until autumn when rain fills up the tanks again.

All Spanish gardeners insist that crops should be sown on the waxing moon, *la luna creciente*. Modern science has confirmed this ancient knowledge by showing that the smallest particle of water anywhere, even in a potato on a laboratory bench, responds to the pull of the moon.

A Choice of Vegetables

Such a variety of vegetables will grow in Spain's superb climate that any garden can only contain a few. Choose those of your own favourites which do best in your particular garden. Rarer varieties will probably have to be raised from seed. For the rest one can sometimes cut a corner by buying boxes of young plants. These are often very good indeed, as local markets are a convenient way for professional growers to dispose of young plants of top quality, but surplus to their own requirements.

Also, very good seeds are sold in Spain. Many supermarkets and garden shops have a wide variety suited to local conditions. Leading international growers market seeds which do well here. The healthy hobby of growing your own vegetables can seldom get off to a better start.

Aubergine or **Egg Plant:** Plant from March to June and expect the harvest in 65-80 days. This ornamental annual vegetable makes a good divider between flower and vegetable gardens. The bushes grow nearly a metre high and equally wide, with big, purple-tinged leaves and violet flowers. They also do well in large containers or raised beds. Plant one metre apart in loose, fertile soil. Feed every six weeks and water when the soil round the plants is dry.

The important point to remember is that the seeds need 27 °C to germinate. (I have done this on a slatted shelf over a hot water tank). They will come through in seven to 14 days. Then transplant into pots and grow in a very light place in the house until the garden soil is warm enough to plant them out.

For large aubergines, prevent too much fruit by pinching out the ends of some stems. For small fruit, allow them to develop freely. Pick after they develop colour, but never wait until the glossy shine has gone.

The Japanese, who like their aubergines tiny and tender, grow yellow varieties which ripen white, and are ideal for stir-fry cooking. These smaller plants grow 55 cm. tall.

Globe Artichoke: A handsome plant about 130 cm. tall, grown for its plump, edible buds. They turn into spectacular flowers like thistles, if left uncut.

Sow seeds in spring 1 cm. deep and thin to 130 cm. apart. In Spanish gardens the plants will live for about seven years. As plants mature, they produce offshoots. Detach and replant in spring (seeing that each has a good supply of roots) to ensure future crops.

If growing dormant roots or container plants, set out in winter or early spring in full sun. Place the roots vertically, with buds or shoots just above the soil. From containers, transfer with as little disturbance as possible at the same soil level. Water well once a week, wetting the whole root-system. If aphids occur, wash them off with a strong jet of water. Avoid pesticides after the buds start to form. Crop very lightly, if at all, the first year.

When the leaves begin to turn yellow, cut off old stalks near to ground level. In mountain gardens, cut down the stems to 30 cm. in autumn, tie them over the crowns and mulch well to protect from frost.

Jerusalem Artichoke: This magnificently tough perennial vegetable is grown from tubers, and produces well even in poor soil. The yellow flowers are like small sunflowers and grow to two metres. Choose a tuber about the size of a hen's egg, or cut up a larger root, making sure that each piece has an "eye". When the leaves turn yellow in autumn, cut down to 30 cm. The crop stores best left in the ground.

Asparagus: Grows well in many different types of soil provided that the land is well-drained. It doesn't need particularly fertile soil, although if you live near the sea and can give a top dressing of seaweed, the results are excellent.

The old-fashioned raised bed produces particularly large spears, but for many years now, good asparagus has been grown on flat beds. As an asparagus bed lasts for years, get rid of perennial weeds before planting. Asparagus can be raised from seed sown thinly in drills in early spring, and transplanted 30 cm. apart the following year. If crowns are available, the programme is put forward by one or two years according to the age of the crowns. Look for large, well-developed crowns at least as big as a man's hand. As they develop, they will produce offshoots which can be replanted. Plant in autumn or winter in warm areas, and in early spring in high or exposed gardens.

To make the bed, dig trenches 30 cm. wide and 20-25 cm. deep, 130 cm. apart. Place loose, rich soil at the bottom of the trenches and wet thoroughly. Set the crowns so that the tops are 15-20 cm. below the surface, 30 cm. apart, spreading out the roots. Cover with 5 cm. of soil, and water again.

As the young plants grow, gradually fill in the trench. Don't cover the growing tips. Soak very thoroughly whenever the soil begins to dry out, and don't harvest any spears the first year. The bigger the plants grow, the more productive they will be in the long run. When the foliage turns brown, cut it down to the ground.

The next year, harvest spears for four to six weeks only, or until thinner growth warns you to give the plants time to recover.

Feed and water well for the rest of the year and keep the bed weed-free. The following year crop for eight to 10 weeks, cutting stems carefully with a sharp knife and making a diagonal cut downwards to avoid damaging adjoining stems.

Broad Beans: Sow where they are to grow, any time from October, and crop from January onwards. Set seeds 5 cm. deep and 20 cm. apart. Broad beans are not a thirsty crop, but water when they come into flower and continue during the pod-forming period. The scent is an added bonus. I have seen broad beans planted in oil drums on each side of the door of a village house — a practical pleasure. In Spain they are seldom troubled with black fly. If this should happen, remove the tips.

French Beans: Sow in spring and well into summer to get a continuous supply. Cultivate the soil until it is light and crumbly to help the seedlings come through. Plant 2 cm. deep every 7 cm. in rows 35 cm. apart. Expect the crop in three months. Keep well picked to get maximum yield.

Runner and Climbing French Beans: Many varieties of seed are on offer of these most productive crops. Provide support such as a tripod of poles, or plant by a sun-trap wall and train up strings or a trellis. Water the ground thoroughly before planting but don't moisten again until the seedlings have come through. From then on keep the ground damp. Feed once when the plants are in active growth, and again when the pods start to form. Cropping starts in 50-70 days, according to the variety. Pick frequently. If the beans mature they grow tough and the plant stops production.

Beetroot: Plant seed directly into the ground where it is to grow. For fresh beet throughout the summer, plant in short rows every four weeks. This crop does best in sun and takes four months to mature. In hot southern gardens, plant to mature before or after extreme heat. Sow seeds 2 cm. apart, covering them with a very light layer of compost or sand. Thin the plants to 5 cm. apart (you can use the thinnings). Water often and feed every three to four weeks for fast, tender growth. Begin harvesting when the beets are 3 cm. in diameter and never let them grow larger than 8 cm. across.

Brussels Sprouts: A familiar crop which is at its best in sierra gardens which get a touch of frost in the winter. Sow from early to mid-spring in an outdoor seed-bed, and plant out very firmly, spacing 60 cm. apart each way. Old gardeners say the best Brussels sprouts are planted with a crowbar.

Cabbage: Comes in many varieties and you can choose one to sow any month. Most Spanish home gardeners sow in spring for autumn and winter use, and in autumn for spring. Sow into a seed-bed. When the plants reach 15 cm., transplant into good soil at a distance of 60 x 70 cm. apart. Keep weed-free and well watered.

Carrot: Sow at any time directly in the place where they are to grow. Carrots grow best in light, rich soil, but will also perform well in very sandy soil provided they are fed. Don't try them in heavy or stony ground. Plant on land (if available) which has already carried brassicas. Sow seeds 1 cm. deep, with the early-crop rows 15 cm. apart, and main-crop rows 20 cm. apart. An eight-metre row should yield about 11 kilos of mature carrots.

Carrots contain more vitamin A than any other vegetables. The best variety to choose depends on the depth of light, friable soil you have. Even gardeners with inhospitable land, or patio gardeners can grow sweet, bright, finger-sized carrots in tubs of peat. For this, choose a short variety such as Suko. Carrots store well in the ground and can be dug as needed.

Land-Cress, sometimes known as **American Land-Cress.** A useful, trouble-free crop to grow in Spain, where true watercress takes attention to grow and is often hard to find. Land-cress has the distinctive watercress flavour, but the plant grows taller and the leaves are rather dryer. Sow thinly in rows from early spring onwards in all but the hottest weather. Thin and use as plants develop. Water well and the cress will be ready in seven to eight weeks. Plants last through the winter.

Seeds may be difficult to find locally but are available from some exporters, including Thompson and Morgan.

Cauliflower: Grow standard cauliflower as cabbages. Try the easy mini-cauliflowers pioneered by the British National Vegetable Research Station. These have the advantages that they can be sown directly into the ground; take up only 15 x 15 cm. each; are useful for small families, and freeze well. Harvest when the head is up to 8 cm. across.

With cauliflowers in particular, comes the problem that they all ripen together. Cope with this by successional sowing. Hold back individuals for a day or two by bending the leaves over the heads.

Cucumber: Choose an outdoor variety even if your climate is very mild, as English indoor types *must* be grown indoors to avoid pollination by bees. Grow as for melons (see previous chapter). Most outdoor varieties will trail, but will be more productive if given a support to climb up. Plant seeds in a sunny spot and keep evenly moist. To grow up a trellis, plant seeds 2 cm. deep and 30-100 cm. apart and let the main stem reach the top. Plant seeds in March, or according to local climate, one to two weeks after the likely date of the last frost. Pick young for maximum flavour and a good crop.

Bush Cucumbers are compact and ideal for growing in small spaces and containers. They yield their first crops remarkably soon after planting; sometimes as quickly as two months.

Gherkin: A form of mini outdoor cucumber. Good varieties produce an immense number of 8-12 cm. long gherkins for pickling or salads.

Courgette or Zucchini: In most areas start off the seeds in a warm place in the house in early spring at 20 °C. Sow seeds singly on edge in 7-cm. pots. Light is not important at this stage. Move to a light, warm position when the seeds have germinated. Harden off gradually and plant out in a sunny site. Provide a humus-rich soil. Never allow it to dry, but keep water off leaves and stems as much as possible. Space plants 60 cm. apart each way. Use courgettes while they are still young and tender.

Leek: Sow seed from February to October in a seed-bed. Then transplant by the unusual but traditional method of making a hole in the ground with a dibber (space 15 cm. apart), dropping in the young leek, then filling up the hole with water without firming the soil. Leeks need very rich earth. Never let it dry completely. When the stems are well grown, draw up the soil to blanch them and improve the flavour — this makes them mild rather than fiery.

Plant out three months after sowing, and expect the crop three months later.

Lettuce: A major salad plant which is very easy to grow. Today a wider-than-ever choice is on offer. "Cut and Come Again" and "All Year Round" varieties are popular. Cos lettuce succeeds well in most gardens. When to plant depends on the local weather and the water available. In hot gardens all varieties are better grown in autumn, winter or spring, with some shade in the hottest hours. Cooler gardens have a longer planting season. Water plentifully, and feed lightly but often. Sow in open ground at 10-day intervals, barely covering the seeds. Expect baby lettuce in 27-48 days. Larger varieties will take four to five months.

Plant lettuces close enough to shade the soil. This way, the soil won't dry out so fast, thus conserving water. As the lettuces come through, thin progressively, using the thinnings. With large varieties aim finally for a lettuce every 30 cm. The recent popularity of red lettuce adds attractive colour to kitchen gardens and subsequent salads.

Sweet Corn: Recent scientific work has revolutionized this crop. Today you can grow varieties which are sweeter (and keep this sweetness for longer) than ever before. The season varies with the region and the types planted. In a year when summer lingered late, I have known sweet corn planted in September to be ripe and delicious the same year.

Normally sow seed from late March in frost-free areas. Elsewhere plant two weeks after the last expected frost. Sow 2 cm. deep where the plants are to grow. Site plants 30-60 cm. apart, setting the plants in blocks, not rows, as the pollen is distributed by wind.

Sweet corn needs a light, sandy soil. If necessary improve yours with coarse sand and peat, at the same time digging in compost or manure, the autumn before you plan to plant. In spring add extra fertilizer.

For sweet, tender corn, grow the crop fast, giving plenty of water, especially between tasselling time and harvest. Thin ruthlessly and keep down weeds with a mulch of compost. Never hoe.

Onion: Spanish onions are famous, as the long, hot summers ripen the bulbs to perfection. Choose an open, well-manured site. Grow from seeds or sets (small bulblets). Sets are easier for the beginner, but seeds are cheaper and always available.

Plant sets in winter, until March or April, 2-3 cm. deep, 10-15 cm. apart in rows 30 cm. apart. Each set should produce an onion weighing at least 170 grams. You can use the space between rows by intercropping with radishes or lettuces.

Most Spanish gardeners sow seed in August or September into a seedbed, and plant out three months later, for a crop which will mature in eight months. This is often followed by another sowing in spring. Sow seeds 1 cm. deep in rows 20 cm. apart and thin plants to 15 cm.

As onions are shallow-rooted, take special care to see that they don't dry out, and feed as the plants develop. When the tops begin to wither, dig up the onions and let them dry on top of the ground for several days. Then remove the tops, clean the onions and store in a cool, dark, airy place. Many country gardeners store their crops by hanging them up in bunches.

Parsnip: A fine, nourishing vegetable which has been grown since ancient times round the Mediterranean. Grow in full sun. Plant seeds in autumn; harvest in spring. Soak seeds for 24 hours before planting, then sow 1 cm. deep in rows 30 cm. apart. Thin the seedlings to 7 cm.

Peas: They prefer to grow in cool weather, so in warm gardens plant peas from October to December directly where they are to grow. They will be ready to eat in two to three months. In cooler gardens plant in early spring, as soon as the ground can be cultivated. Sow 5 cm. deep in light, moisture-retentive soil. In winter, or if soil is heavy, put seeds only 1-2 cm. deep. Water the ground well before planting, then don't water again until the seedlings have come through. Space rows 60 cm. apart and thin seedlings to a distance of 5 cm.

The most productive varieties are the tall climbers, which must have sticks, strings or other support, as soon as the tendrils show. If you haven't got the space, or don't want the work of fixing supports, grow the bush type which can manage without help.

Stagger sowings to avoid a glut. The reward of growing your own, is the delicious taste of young, fresh peas, which have been picked and served in a matter of hours. Take off all fully ripe peas whether you need them or not, as if left, the plant will stop production.

Peas grow well on ground which has previously held brassicas.

Sweet Pepper: An easy crop to grow. Sow seed early in the year or buy plants between March and May and irrigate well, but not often. The plants are bushy, 50-60 cm. tall. Grow in full sun, spacing plants 20 cm. apart. Eat peppers while green, or wait until they turn red when fully mature.

Chilli Peppers: According to the United States Department of Agriculture, and also the University of California, red-hot pepper contains a formidable list of health-giving minerals and vitamins, including iron and vitamin C.

Grow red-hot peppers for drying — *chili serrano* is a good variety — in pots standing against a sunny wall but protected from rain. A patio or terrace is ideal. Plant in spring, 2 cm. deep in potting soil. When mature, sun-dry or store in damp salt. In really hot gardens, grow in the open as a perennial. The plants last three years.

Spinach: A crop to grow at home, as it wilts quickly and often looks tired in markets. Good seed is sold locally, suitable for prevailing conditions. One variety can be sown for most of the year except in spring. (The aim is to avoid having plants trying to grow during the heat of summer. You can sow seed in summer to be growing in autumn.) Grow in short rows 30 cm. apart and repeat frequently for an onflow crop. Thin plants to 10 cm. apart. Give fertile, well-drained, friable soil. Make summer sowings in a site which gets little direct sun. Water well, and the ambient heat will help the plants to develop quickly.

Potato: Usually sown twice a year, in December and August, in the place where they are to grow, they will be ready to eat in approximately five months. In frost-free gardens it is possible to manage three crops a year, but the consensus is that two crops do better. Grow on the same patch for one year, then rotate the crop to a site which has grown brassicas. Even if precise rotation is difficult, don't grow one root-crop after another in the same place.

Potatoes are valuable food, and also help to improve the land by fighting perennial weeds. Buy the best seed potatoes you can get. If you prefer to cut up seed potatoes, see that each piece you plant has two "eyes".

Potatoes need sandy, fast-draining soil and grow in two directions at once, sending shoots both down and upwards. Young potatoes form on the upward-growing shoot, so encourage it to be as long as possible by "earthing up". Do this every fortnight for six weeks, so that only the top of the green shoots show. Plant 15 cm. deep every 30 cm., in rows 75 cm. apart. After the top growth appears, water occasionally but well. Grow in full sun.

Dig up new potatoes when the flowers start. These are for immediate use and won't keep. Dig mature potatoes when the tops die down. Storage time varies, but kept in sawdust, potatoes last well for two months.

As a rough guide, half a kilo of seed potatoes will produce about four to nine kilos of potatoes, according to the variety and growing conditions. Even 15 seed potatoes can produce a harvest of 18-23 kilos. Always grow tubers covered with earth. Parts exposed to light turn green and should not be eaten.

Sweet Potato: A staple crop in southern areas. Best on warm, well-drained, sandy loam soils. Make rows one metre apart and ditch between them to form ridges 20 cm. high. Plant the sweet potatoes 15 cm. deep and 40 cm. apart on the ridges, with only the tips showing. Once growing well, there is no need to water. Plant and harvest according to the accepted time in your area. Remember that this greatly loved vegetable needs a long growing season; does take up space, and is difficult to store well. Most growers dry them in the sun and eat the crop as soon as possible.

Radish: It is a delight to pull a bunch of shining, red radishes and use them at once — fresh, crisp and spicy. They need plenty of water and good soil. For best results grow as fast as possible, don't overcrowd and eat as soon as they reach acceptable size. The fastest radishes are ready in three weeks from sowing. The slowest are the long varieties, white or black, such as Long Black Spanish, which takes about two months. Grow in full sun in early spring and autumn, and in light shade in warmer weather. Avoid hottest months. Sow seeds 2 cm. deep and thin to 2 cm. apart when top growth appears. Rows are convenient at 30 cm. although Spanish country gardeners grow splendid radishes by broadcasting seed.

Tomato: Although strictly-speaking a fruit, the tomato is more commonly thought of as a vegetable. In spite of the fine tomatoes on sale in shops and markets, enthusiastic tomato growers (and eaters) often prefer to grow their own. They are so much easier to produce in Spain than in colder countries where many of us first learned to grow our crops. Exciting varieties are available to the home gardener, such as tiny, cherry-sized fruits for salads; yellow tomatoes; semi-bush types, very suitable for growing in planters on patios and balconies — they need no staking until the trusses get so heavy you have to give them a helping hand — and that favourite with nearly everyone, plum tomatoes. These grow abundantly here, but are often unavailable to the retail trade as crops are snapped up by the canning industry.

Many gardeners achieve two crops a year, one sown in spring for summer use, and one sown in summer for use in winter.

Sow seeds into a box or prepared seed-bed in January or February, and plant out into the final position two months later. You may prefer to buy plants ready to set out in April or May, cutting out the seedling stage.

Grow tomatoes up a tripod of sticks or any other convenient support. You will have to tie them in, as having no tendrils, they cannot climb by themselves. Choose a sunny position in fertile, well-drained soil, planting 50 cm. apart.

In all but bush varieties watch vigilantly for side-shoots forming in the axil between leaf and stem, which takes strength from the plant. Water well and often (the roots go deep) and feed with a special tomato or other high-nitrogen fertilizer once a fortnight from the time of first flowering.

Small-fruited tomatoes can be planted in a hanging basket and allowed to cascade down.

The second crop is also most useful. Sow at the end of May or early June into seed-trays or beds. Prick out and plant in the final position at the end of August or in September. Tomatoes come about November, and continue throughout the winter. For all sowings choose a tomato suited to your climate. The variety Alicante does particularly well for autumn/winter croppings in most areas.

If you expect frost, harvest all fruit at once, whether ripe, partly ripe or green. Green tomatoes can be ripened in the house or made into chutney.

Gardening
in Special Situations

By the Sea

 ardens by the sea have special advantages. Above all there is the view, which is probably why you chose the site in the first place. But certain limitations are imposed by the salt breezes, depending in degree on the exposure of each particular garden.

Many trees, shrubs and flowers stand up well to these conditions. Here is a list of some of the most useful. It is not definitive. Given a little protection many other favourites will grow also.

Trees

Tamarisk with its airy pink flowers stands up to sea air and positively relishes salt in the soil.

Palm will grow in sea sand a few metres from the high-water mark, but don't attempt it in gardens where strong, cold winds are frequent. Some public plantings have failures because mature trees are planted with over-pruned roots. Plant your palm tree young, so that the supporting and nourishing roots develop fully as the tree grows.

Pine and **cypress** also do well by the sea. In wind-swept conditions choose the dark, narrowly columnar Italian cypress. It makes little opposition to the blast and I have never known one blow over.

Fig will flourish and fruit within sound of the waves.

Olive grows well close to the water's edge. Surprisingly an olive tree will stand clipping and still bear fruit.

Eucalyptus. A beautiful, fast-growing tree. Don't plant too many as they demand much from the soil, robbing other plants. Buy from a local grower. He will stock the varieties which like coastal conditions.

Holm-Oak. A Mediterranean native whose English name means sea oak. Best (and cheapest) grown from an acorn, as oaks do not like to be transplanted.

Shrubs

Sea-resistant shrubs decorate the garden and where necessary provide protection.

Spanish Broom, Spartium, grows two to three metres high, producing its scented yellow flowers from April or May to about the end of August.

Pampas-Grass makes good-looking, substantial clumps of arching, narrow leaves, throwing up plumes of dusty pink or cream at the end of summer. Fine plants, both decorative and protective.

Pittosporum. A decorative bush covered with sweet-scented, cream blossom in spring. In some situations it blooms again in September.

Myporum, with its dark, glossy leaves and small white flowers, is extremely hardy and undemanding. Grow it as a bush, trimming well to shape, or as a street hedge against an iron railing. Clip protruding branches for a well-groomed effect.

Agave, with its handsome corona of green and cream leaves, is one of the classic sights of the Mediterranean coast. After some years the flower-spike emerges like a great pole, rising up to six metres high. Yellow flowers are borne in flat groups like "hands", followed by much seed. The agave then dies. Often offsets cluster round the parent. This dramatic plant looks particularly at home among rocks or on a sea cliff.

Sea Tomato, Rosa Rugosa. This tough, fragrant, open rose flourishes in windy and sea-spray conditions, producing round, red hips like tomatoes. Train as hedge or allow to form mounds.

Flowers

Sea Lavender, Limonium, grows wild by the shore and has been improved by seedsmen to produce larger flowers and bright colours, including crimson, yellow and white. Splendid in the garden and one of the best for dried flower arrangements.

Geranium. All kinds do well, but if conditions are difficult, choose the ivy-leaved geranium which will climb, or is splendid as flowering ground cover.

Ice-Plant, Carpobrotus. Plant for bright carpets of ground cover. Loves sand and seaside places.

Daisy Bush, *Chrysanthemum frutescens.* Grow in full sun and light soil. These comparatively short-lived perennial bushes do exceptionally well near the coast and cover themselves with white daisies.

Aloe, fleshy and succulent with flowers like red-hot pokers, and the silver-leaved sea **cineraria** always perform well.

For sweeps of colour and for cutting, plant **Californian poppies marigolds** and **cornflowers**.

For a special treat try to find the white **sea-daffodil**. It grows wild on sand-dunes by the sea from a bulb which often lies deep in dry places. In July and August come pure white daffodils with a wonderful perfume. Avon Bulbs hold stocks, also Van Tubergen of Holland (see pages 188 &189).

Gardening on a Slope

Gardening on a steep slope has one particular problem — you need to keep the soil in place. Erosion by garden watering or rain can send valuable soil cascading down the hillside. The problem can be solved in two ways: either by terracing, or by introducing plants which stabilize the soil. You may want to use both methods in different parts of the garden. It is also important if you occasionally experience torrential rains to make escape channels for excess water.

Terracing

Making terraces is the traditional method of getting the best out of a steep hillside plot. Gardeners in steep situations, as on the Rock of Gibraltar, for instance, make skilful use of this method.

The hillside is cut out into "steps", traditionally shored up with stone walls. This produces a series of flat beds on which crops and flowers can be grown, the flat beds preventing soil loss.

Today some gardeners shore up their terraces with timber, such as old railway sleepers or solid planks. Treat wood with preservative before putting into place.

The series of flat beds has the added advantage that it gives a fine view of your flowers, and often protects from wind. It also enables you to grow flopping plants such as creeping rosemary, ivy-leaved geraniums or russelia hanging over the edge of each terrace.

Stabilize Your Soil with Plants

On slopes where you don't want to terrace, use plants whose deep roots will hold the soil.

Tall Fescue is a tall (75 cm.), coarse-growing grass excellent for erosion control in difficult situations as the roots go deep. Sow generously as this grass makes no runners. For full erosion control do not mow. Many *viveros* also supply grass seed mixtures suitable for more moderate erosion control. If not in stock, these can be obtained for you through trade catalogues.

Rock-Rose. Sun-loving, rock-roses flourish and prevent earth slippage. An added bonus is the flush of eye-catching flowers in spring. Water carefully (gentle drip irrigation is excellent) until the shrubs are fully established. In two to three years they will provide some slope protection. In four to six years they will be fully established. Meanwhile you can interplant with ice-plants for ground cover.

Rosa Rugosa is helpful in the fight against soil erosion. Also the scented, open roses are showy, and the round, tomato-like hips ("edible but seedy," say those who have tried them) give notable secondary interest in autumn.

Mimosa and **Acacia.** In warm areas these beautifully flowered (but not very long-lived) trees have taken to the hills of Spain and decorate and protect southern slopes.

Gorse. Spiny evergreen shrubs with golden flowers which come mainly in spring. Some appear all year round, giving rise to the old saying, "When gorse is out of bloom, kissing is out of fashion." Gorse does not transplant well. Grow from seed in spring, preferably sown where you want the bushes; or for the double sort, which doesn't set seed, plant firm, young cuttings in early summer. Clip for shape as necessary in spring.

Unthirsty Plants for Dry Places

Demand for water grows each year, so in most gardens it is useful to have a number of unthirsty plants. In some it is essential.

Where water has to be used with care, it often pays to concentrate the available supply on particular areas, and grow there the plants that need it. In other places, have interesting and beautiful trees, bushes and flowers that have adapted to doing well on very little moisture.

Trees

Fig. The best figs grow hard in dry places. Over-careful growers can actually reduce the flavour of the crop by pampering it. In particular, water given as the fruit is setting results in mushy figs.

Olive, Pine and **Oak.** Old as Mediterranean history, olives thrive in places where watering is impossible, as do pines and oaks. It is only necessary to get the young (or mature, transplanted) trees established in the first place, for them to survive on natural rainfall.

False Pepper Tree, Schinus. A good-looking tree with feathery foliage and seeds that do indeed look like peppers. Don't attempt to eat them. Allow this tree plenty of room and it will look beautiful and give shade for sitting under.

Yucca. Fine trees with sharp leaves and huge white, lily-like flowers. If possible have several in the garden.

Locust Tree, Robinia. A deciduous tree with clusters of white or pink "sweet-pea" flowers in early summer. Prune well after the summer season, especially in its early years.

Carob, Ceratonia, sometimes also called the Locust tree. By tradition the tree whose seeds John the Baptist lived on during his stay in the wilderness. Allowed to grow naturally, it is covered with branches to the ground and often multi-stemmed. In this form, use it as a large hedge, informal or trimmed. Trained as a tree, with lower branches removed, it can reach six metres in 10 years, with thick, dark-green, sparkling leaves. Female carobs look spectacular with their dark brown pods 30 cm. long hanging from the branches.

Shrubs

Spanish Broom. Grow in full sun and prune if the shrub becomes too tall and thin.

Jade Plant, Crassula. A splendid succulent for dry gardens, either in a container or the open ground. Grows slowly with thick, silvery-grey stems and small green leaves, later bearing pink star flowers. Remarkably drought-resistant. Will eventually reach up to three metres. Very easy to propagate from small cuttings rooted in water.

Matilija Poppy, Romneya. It is always surprising that this spectacular shrub supports dry conditions and poor, stony soil. A native of southern California and Mexico, the scented, papery white poppy flowers with their centres of bright golden stamens are 20 cm. across and come in June and July. For indoor arrangements cut the blooms in bud. They will open in water and last for several days. Don't place Romneya near less vigorous plants, as this shrub spreads by underground runners and is invasive.

Firethorne an evergreen shrub with small, creamy flowers and bright berries. Tolerates a good deal of drought, but does better with occasional watering in summer. When you do water, water deeply.

Lion's Ear, Leonotis. A striking shrub growing one to two metres tall, with whorls of orange flowers growing up the stems. Plant in full sun.

Rock-Rose. One of the wild shrubs of Spain, growing naturally in dry places.

Flowers

Choose flowers which can get by with little or no watering and you will have colour in the garden without problems. **Nasturtium,** the silver-leaved **cineraria maritima, sea lavender, rosemary** — there's a creeping type as well — **thyme,** the white **sea-daffodil** and a huge variety of **cacti** and succulents are all most suitable for growing in dry places.

The Absentee Gardener

PAIN is a compelling country and draws people from all over the world. Although for many the new land becomes home, for others a house in the sun is only an intermittent pleasure.

Long periods away can cause problems in the garden, but you can make the best of the situation, whether your plot is a rolling hillside, a patio or a few planters on a balcony.

Exactly what are your assets and what are the problems? The sooner you identify them the more successful you will be. Bear in mind too that for gardeners Spain is a forgiving country. Even if a garden is neglected, once you can give it attention it is surprising how soon it can be returned to its full glory.

First consider the climate, which varies considerably in different regions of the Iberian peninsula and the Spanish islands. Note the type of soil, winds and how much water is available. Next, make as fair an estimate as possible as to how often you will be present.

If money isn't a problem, seek out an experienced local *vivero* owner and come to an arrangement with him both to supply plants and maintain your garden. Tell him what you want — this can be an ongoing dialogue as you fall in love with more and more plants and flowers. I know several conscientious men always on the alert that "their" owners may arrive at any time, and that the gardens in their care must always look inviting.

If yours is a tight budget, act accordingly. A cheaper, simpler garden for the present, filled with plants that succeed easily, brings more pleasure than an over-ambitious planting scheme that won't stay the course. Don't have a lawn if you are not sure you can maintain it.

Defend the Perimeter
Mark out the boundaries of your property and enclose them with a fence or hedge. Unmarked boundaries can wander, and encroachment is easier to prevent than to deal with later. If you are not sure what to grow, walk round the area and see what plants are already growing well there.

Soil
Often Spanish soil is good, or at least adequate. Then you need only budget for enough manure annually to maintain or improve it.

Where soil is very poor some gardeners cover the whole of their land with 25 cm. of rich earth. At the other end of the scale I know a young couple who built their house on a bare hilltop. They bought soil from building sites and brought it up the mountain, sackful by sackful, in the boot of their car. Flower-beds were constructed one at a time. Today that garden is a delight. It may take longer, but hard work and persistence can bring splendid results.

Water
The most fortunate gardeners have supplies of free water on site such as a well, or sometimes the benefit of irrigation schemes built by the Arabs which still function perfectly. But for most people water is a commodity which has to be paid for. Economize as necessary by choosing unthirsty plants and making the best of the water you use.

The most thrifty method is to buy narrow-gauge drip irrigation tubes and snake them about the garden so that they deliver water slowly just where it is most needed. The pipes can be connected to a garden tap controlled manually or, more expensively, to an automated system. The

disadvantage of the manual scheme is that it works perfectly while you are present, but when you are away it may prove too time-consuming to monitor for any help you can enlist.

The best bet may be to get a gardener or maid to water your garden or planters once a week with a hose-pipe.

Also remember to mulch any newly-planted tree or shrub with peat, bark or compost. Water the subject well, put on the mulch and then water again. In this way the roots of the plant are kept cool and damp for as long as possible.

Shelter

All gardens, even the windiest, have some shelter. There is the mass of the house itself to provide differing micro-climates, and this shelter from sun and wind can be supplemented by walls, hedges and plantings of trees and shrubs.

Lawns

An important decision must be made with regard to an absentee-owned garden. Lawn or no lawn?

If you decide on a lawn, it will need some maintenance. A beautiful lawn of pedigree grass must be fully cared for in your absence with regular watering, mowing and feeding. If you want a sweep of green grass but are prepared to settle for a hardier lawn, plant the local *grama* grass, which can be mowed with a rotary cutter; can survive on less water, and get by with very little attention.

Plants for the Absentee-Owned Garden

Trees

Trees are the main architectural points of a garden, giving interest and shade. Bear in mind as you plan, that trees grow in width as well as height, and allow enough space. Plant trees well away from walls, drains and water-pipes, as roots can be invasive.

Every tree newly planted will need care for about a year before it is fully established. If possible be present at the planting, or leave it with someone you can trust implicitly. Arrange for suitable watering and then, on your subsequent visits, check that the tree is still firmly in the ground and properly tied and staked.

Among the best survivors are **yucca** with its huge, gleaming white blooms; **palm** — after a year or two take advice on pruning away the lowest branches to form the columnar trunk; **olive** — ancient as Mediterranean history, and bearing a rich crop of fruit; **fig** which grows anywhere; **almond** for its clouds of blossom in early spring and later the crop of nuts; **pepper,** schinus — this shady, feathery tree is a *false* pepper and the fruits are not edible; **cypress,** tall, dark and self-sufficient; **lemon** — choose the "lunar" variety which blossoms and fruits every month; the trouble-free **Seville orange,** with keen-scented blossom in spring followed by golden globes, and the swiftly-growing **eucalyptus.**

Buy one or two varieties of **mimosa,** planned to flower at different times of the year, or the **bottle-brush,** callistemon. Give water when you can, but it will survive drought, as does the **pomegranate. Pine** trees stand up to difficult conditions such as poor soil and sea winds, as does the airy **tamarisk,** with its blue-green leaves and pinkish blossom.

Shrubs and Climbers

Plant flowering shrubs and climbers as one of the most rewarding ways of decorating the garden.

Sturdy **lantana** with its long flowering season is tremendous value for space. Also hardy and reliable are **mock orange,** philadelphus, smothered in blossom in May; lovely **oleander** and **hibiscus; pampas-grass,** cortaderia, which blooms at the end of summer, and the Christmas-flowering **poinsettia.**

Flash colour up into another dimension with flowering climbers. Among the hardiest are **bougainvillaea** — be prepared to prune it hard once a year; **wistaria** with its breath-taking bloom on the bare branches of spring, later protectively shady in leaf on a pergola in high summer. Try pink **bignonia,** attractive and very easy to grow; pale blue **plum-**

bago or the orange **Cape honeysuckle.** If you are likely to visit your Spanish garden three or four times in the year and have a sunny wall to cover, plant the **Cup-of-Gold vine**, solandra. This fast-growing climber produces spectacular flowers of yellowish orange, which often smell of apricots. Its beautiful and rapid growth (up to five metres in 12 months) means that it must be pruned and trained regularly for ideal results.

One of the most economical of all climbers is ipomoea or **morning glory**. Sow seeds in spring near anything it can climb up and it will reseed itself every year, appearing unexpectedly in the most attractive way.

Flowers, herbs and succulents

Fill borders with perennials which will always be there to greet you when you come to your second home. White-flowered **daisy bushes** *Chrysanthemum frutescens;* **gazania,** the treasure flower, with its big, coloured daisy blooms; **echium, iris** and **Livingstone daisies** are all prepared to bear your absence with fortitude.

Plant bulbs such as **narcissi** and **daffodils**. Add **freesias** and **bluebells**. If your **belladonna lilies** fail to appear on time in August, flood the site with water. The subsequent sudden appearance of rosy flowers is dramatic.

Rosemary and **lavender** bring aromatic scent, while **cacti** and succulents are nearly indestructible. Try rosettes of the **Canary Island aeonium** with its bold yellow flower-heads. **Aloes** like red-hot pokers, burn through the winter. Don't do without the dramatic **agave**. After a few years the fine clump of greyish leaves sends up a great pole which bears on its upper branches greenish-yellow flowers — one of the evocative sights of the Mediterranean.

Very many more readily available plants do well in a garden whose owners must often be away. One tip worth knowing while you are still unfamiliar with the Spanish names of plants: when you go to the garden centre, take along with you photographs of the plants you wish to buy.

Clothe the ground, reduce weeds and, where necessary, stabilize banks by the use of ground-cover plants. Purple **creeping lantana** stands up to neglect and flowers practically all the year. Evergreen **periwinkle** needs some shade and a little water but will be with you always, flowering in spring and early summer. **Ivy-leaved geraniums** are true assets, covering the ground with flowers. They will wait between one visit and the next to be trained where you want them to go.

Make use of the large family of mesembryanthemum with their fleshy leaves and brilliant, daisy-like flowers. All do well in hot, dry places and are ideal for the absentee gardener. **Portulaca** opens its brilliant flowers when the sun shines and closes them as shadows fall. It is an annual, sown where it is to flower, but readily self-seeds. **Ice-plants** and **carpobrotus** are other members of this tough and decorative family of succulents.

Gardening
for The Disabled

 N recent years there has been a marked increase of interest in
gardening for the disabled. I have met many disabled gardeners who have been clever enough to get round the problems of
gardening in spite of various disabilities.

Bad backs are often the trouble and can be much helped by the use of
raised flower beds. One keen rock gardener built a raised bed about one
metre high beside a pleasant path. The growing area was not too wide
— about 60 cm. across — so that all work could be done in comfort standing on the path, at an easy height and without too much stretching.

For people confined to a wheelchair, the Royal Horticultural Society of
England has built a special demonstration area in its gardens at Wisley,
Surrey. Here paths have been paved and are wide enough to take a chair

easily. The beds are raised to table height, retained by brick walls, and can be comfortably approached from all sides. They are also built small enough to be within the stretching distance of a chair-borne gardener.

The cost of a paved garden can be reduced by using concrete, which can come in the form of sets, flags or bricks. But always remember to keep the paths wide enough to permit a wheelchair to be easily managed and, of course, no steps. If necessary their place can be taken by ramps.

The range of flowers and vegetables that can be grown is surprising. Brussels sprouts, cabbages, dwarf beans, strawberries, salads, and many more varieties, plain or exotic, are easily manageable in such a "kitchen garden".

The other beds — especially here in Spain — can produce an infinite variety of flowers. Almost the only plants to be avoided are climbers, trees and large bushes.

Yet some problems may remain. Mrs Wendy Kemish, manning a stand from her wheelchair at the Chelsea Flower Show in London, gave me further advice. She had been in a chair for 30 years and gardening for the last 20, and spoke from experience.

"See that the rims of your raised beds are wide enough to sit on," she told me. "This is a great help." Have the raised beds tailored to your particular needs. Some people prefer beds one metre high, others 60 cm. or even less.

Straight-sided beds are excellent — up to a point. But try leaning forward or sideways to reach them from a chair and the physical strain may be too much.

At the Nuffield Orthopaedic Centre in Oxford, special attention has been given to the needs of disabled gardeners.

In their purpose-built garden, raised beds flanked by handrails embody ideas from many sources, including a permanently fixed hose-pipe which is wound and unwound by manual controls.

For many years the Nuffield Foundation has given thought to suitable gardening tools. Today they have come up with a selection of about 20 tools, all in commercial production, which have proved to be the most popular with disabled gardeners. The right weight, length and comfortable grip have been thoroughly tested. For the list, write to: David Hollinrake, Mary Marlborough Lodge, Nuffield Orthopaedic Centre, Windmill Road, Headington, Oxford, England.

A winning entry of the *Sunday Times* "Wheelchair Garden Competition" was built for the Chelsea Flower Show several years ago. The designer, Andrew Neil, was particularly able to appreciate the problems as his wife is confined to a wheelchair.

The winning entry had beds made from old floor-boards raised on legs so that the knees of the chair-borne gardener could fit underneath, like a typist at a table. They were built with the floor sloping downwards to give a greater depth of earth in the centre for those plants that need it, and surrounded by a specially-constructed rim. "Just what I need to support my arms while my hands do the work," said Mrs Neil.

For blind people, an interesting development is information recorded on cassettes by various specialist flower societies, such as the British Fuchsia Society.

A gardener who has been blind all her life told me that she can smell the perfume of those fuchsia flowers which are usually thought to be without scent, and with her super-sensitive fingers can detect flowers, buds and the shape and vigour of the plant. She can sometimes even tell by touch the fertilizer that has been used. "If the veins are protruding on the back of the leaf it means that the plant has been fed with fertilizer with a high nitrogen content," she said.

Both gardeners who can see and those who cannot should try some of the wonderful scented flowers and aromatic plants which do so well in Spain: catmint, thyme and lavender, datura for hot nights (the bushes bloom for an unbelievably long period from the end of spring until the New Year, but the best of the scent comes with the summer nights). Never plant a rose that is not fragrant. Remember narcissi, natives of the Mediterranean. Plant irises and scented lilies.

An unexpected pleasure was the garden built by the London Association for the Blind (14-16 Verney Road, London SE16 3DZ, England) at a Chelsea Flower Show some years ago. Under the title "The Scented Glade", perfumed plants were understandably emphasized, such as the aromatic herbs, mint, thyme and rosemary.

The partially-sighted were also catered for by splashes of easy-to-see, bright colour, given by spirea, azalea, marigolds and geraniums.

All the senses are vitally important, say these experts. A tinkling fountain gives pleasure to the ear. Different textures of brick are used underfoot to indicate the approach to seats. But the feature that attracted constant attention was a tactile plant — a plant to feel, not to look at. Named *Helichrysum petiolatum* it has no common name, and is not the same as the straw flower, also called helichrysum, which is dried as an "everlasting" flower.

This helichrysum is a low shrub with trailing branches covered with whitish, woolly leaves — pleasant enough, though not spectacular. But run your hands over those leaves, and you receive an almost unbelievable sense of peace and delight.

Give it sun (it has the advantage of being an unthirsty plant), provide sandy soil and trim the branches if they grow too long.

Grow big clumps of clove carnations with their rich perfume. See that you have one or more mimosa trees and their soft scent will suddenly waft on the breeze at the most unlikely times of the year. Philadelphus in May and chrysanthemums in December each have their own unmistakable scent, marking the cycle of the year.

Disabled gardeners should spoil themselves a little with good equipment to suit their own particular needs. Many blind enthusiasts find a Braille thermometer invaluable. And one lover of lawns who seriously damaged a knee in a motor accident, says that he never finds walking so easy and pleasant as when strolling behind a good motor-mower, sniffing the scent of newly-cut grass.

The Junior Gardener

 VERY one of us teaching our children to garden, is sowing seeds of happiness for the future. Gardening shouldn't be a chore. It's fun. Given half a chance, that's the way the younger generation sees it.

Children are fierce individualists with a strong sense of possession, and enjoy planting things all by themselves in their very own gardens. Give them a patch of good ground: it may be a real sacrifice to hand over a prime plot with good soil in an open situation, but who can grow anything in deep shade, or in the starved earth beneath a hedge? Battling against impossible odds could put anyone off gardening for life.

With the site decided, let them grow exactly what they like, even if their ideas don't fit in with your own overall plans. They may want to mark off their boundaries with distinctive edging — bright, white stones, perhaps, where you had dreamed of subtle sweeps of colour — but in all matters of taste the choice must be theirs. Only give advice on actual matters of fact.

You can help enormously by making things available and giving them ideas to choose from, and you can all garden along together.

I still remember the first tree I ever planted. In very early childhood my mother took me into the garden and we each solemnly planted an acorn. With fascination I watched my young oak tree grow way above my head, and what pride there was when it grew taller than my mother's.

A good, big seed makes a satisfactory beginning. **Sunflowers** are excellent if you have room. It is also fun to start with a **lemon** pip. Plant several, each in its own small pot, and keep well watered. When the little trees are 20 cm. high, plant them out in the garden.

Nasturtiums have big seeds too, and are even easier to manage, Just pop them in where they are to grow. Choose a dwarf variety, then the children will have neat plants covered with brilliant flowers, and have the satisfaction of knowing that they grew them all by themselves.

Marigold, **candytuff**, **clarkia** and **love-in-a-mist** are all suitable for beginner gardeners. Or you can try **stocks**, **mignonette, morning glory** or **runner beans**, which ramp up their poles almost as quickly as the beanstalk in the fairy-tale.

Gourds are fun to grow. You can get a packet of mixed seeds with resulting fruits of all shapes and sizes. Remember that they are not for eating.

First soak the seeds for 48 hours in warm water. Then pop them into the ground against a fence or wall so that their tops are covered by about 1.25 cm. of earth. Mark the spots by sticks in the soil.

When the shoots come through, they will twine up the sticks and flower. Then come the strange-looking gourds: hooked, round, shaped like bottles or covered with lumps. Leave them on the plants till the end of summer. They will be quite hard now and you can pick and use them in many ways. You can paint and wax them for decoration, bore holes in them and turn them into musical instruments, or cut off the tops for pots. Children could make nearly all their Christmas presents out of gourds they have grown themselves.

What is important, is to choose something with a high success rate, which does not take too long to show signs of life.

Some families prefer to go to a nursery garden and buy a fruit bush or tree which is already established. The *viveros* sell grafted trees which are bred to crop well.

A lemon tree one metre high, for instance, can be expected to fruit the following year. **Oranges, figs** and **apricots** are other possibilities.

If a child owns a tree and has helped to plant it, he or she will watch with interest the first blossom, followed by tiny green fruit which gradually get big enough to eat. What matters is the sense of personal property.

Take a look round the local nurseries for named **roses.** You may be able to locate the namesake of one of your children. Perhaps you will be able to find the pretty, pale-pink miniature rose "Antonia", which occurred unexpectedly in the garden of a famous rose-grower, and was named after his eldest grandchild.

Other possibilities are "Bettina" and "Just Joey", the tall, flame-coloured "Alexander", "Heidi", or the little yellow floribunda "Kim". Every year new names come up. When it comes to buying, take your child along to choose his own personalized rose.

For the boy's name Charles — and for Scots, young historians and romantics in general — perhaps you can find the double white "Prince Charlie's Rose", the Jacobite rose descended from a cutting of the original bush that Bonnie Prince Charlie sent back in 1760 from the Hague to Flora MacDonald, to thank her for her help in bringing him "Over the Sea to Skye".

Girls and boys just starting school soon learn to spell their names. Give each child a packet of **cress,** a plate and some blotting paper or flannel. Help them to wet the growing medium. They can then "write" their initials or whole names with seed. In a few days the cress will sprout and grow tall, ready to eat in a sandwich. The letters may be wobbly, but it's all great fun.

Another form of garden namesmanship is to let young children plant **marrow** seeds. Teach them to watch for the young marrows forming behind the yellow flowers, and then scratch their names on them and watch them swell. As the marrow grows, so does the name, until it is as bold as a poster.

Teenaged boys — and girls — are often interested in machinery, and a keen 13-year-old can handle a power-driven scythe or lawn-mower with more skill and verve than many non-mechanically-minded adults.

With some machinery an element of risk exists, but teach a responsible child to use equipment properly, and he will soon handle it with expertise.

Will this mechanized gardening lead to proper gardening later on? The chances are that it will. Messing about in gardens is a bug that once caught never quite disappears.

Children of most ages like bulbs, as with minimum care they almost never fail.

A **hyacinth** in a glass will grow in water alone. Keep the level of water just below the bottom of the bulb, and put in a small piece of charcoal to keep it sweet. It doesn't have to go in the dark either. Day by day, the owner can watch the first white roots emerge, followed by the upward-thrusting green shoot which later discloses the flower spike.

Don't buy a top-sized bulb as the heavy flower may crash over: Smaller bulbs are more suitable.

The autumn-flowering meadow saffron, **colchicum,** is an oddity which needs no care at all. Put the bulb on a dry saucer in the light and leave it alone. The flowers will burst from the dry bulb. One of the best varieties for growing dry is the pink-purple "Byzantium". Later on plant it in the garden and it will flower for years.

As you teach your children to garden, teach them about poisonous plants.

No responsible parents would leave their children ignorant of the dangers of eating any parts of unknown wild plants, and this same caution applies to plants in the garden.

Be careful and thorough, but don't go overboard. Are you worried about potatoes or tomatoes? The leaves of both are potentially harmful, although actual cases of poisoning are uncommon, practically to the point of non-existence.

You can't get round the problem by growing only plants that are totally safe, as your children won't always be at home. Teach them about poisonous plants and teach them plant-caution in general. Let them learn thoroughly, and they will be safe wherever they go.

Extremely Poisonous Plants

Arum; castor oil plant — the large, mottled, shiny seeds are poisonous; colchicum; datura; delphinium; hellebore; laburnum — all parts, especially the seeds; oleander — don't use wood for barbecue skewers or for fires, as smoke can cause severe irritation; sweet pea — particularly the seeds; thevetia, tobacco plant; yew.

Poisonous Plants

Anemone; aquilegia; bluebell; box; bracken; clematis; convolvulus — the seeds; cyclamen; dumb cane — gets its common name from the fact that the sap irritates mouth and throat and may paralyse the vocal chords; Dutchman's pipe; euphorbia; flax; holly — the berries carry the poison; hyacinth; iris; ivy; lantana — again the berries; laurel; lily; lobelia; narcissus; poinsettia — a form of euphorbia whose juice is also an irritant; privet; prunus — includes cherry laurel, Portuguese laurel, peach, apricot and almond. The leaves and seeds of all are poisonous. Robinia, the locust tree; senecio — includes cineraria and dusty miller; solanum — includes the Jerusalem cherry (whose unripe berries are particularly dangerous) and also the climbing potato vine and Costa Rican nightshade; tulip and wistaria — especially the seeds.

Shopping By Post

VERY good garden material can be bought in Spain. Trees, bushes, plants and seeds are all available from shops and *viveros,* in good variety and quality.

Yet keen gardeners today, as keen gardeners have always done for hundreds of years, seek out extra pleasure by importing special treasures from overseas.

Abroad

The following firms are prepared to deal with orders from Spain. Details are correct at time of writing but may have changed when you decide to order. Write for latest particulars.

Avon Bulbs, Burnt House Farm, Mid Lambrook, South Petherton, Somerset TA13 5HE, England. Bulbs only. No minimum order. Consignment fee £5.

With this small, individual firm you have the satisfaction of dealing directly with the owner. The stated aim of the company is: "The provision of rare and unusual subjects to keen gardeners."

I found particularly interesting their collection of bulbs for summer flowering. Collections, owing to lower handling charges, give special value for money. The collection for the cool greenhouse will, in most areas of Spain, grow unprotected on the patio or in the garden.

Avon Bulbs offer a good choice of lilies and are one of the very few firms offering the Spanish sea-daffodil, *Pancratium maritimum* which grows wild in the sands of the coastal areas of Andalusia, producing white, keenly-scented flowers at the end of July.

Bloms Bulbs, Coombelands Nurseries, Leavesden, Watford, Herts WD2 7BH, England. Tel. (0923) 672071. Bulbs only. No minimum order.

This family firm has been growing bulbs for over 115 years. Ronald Blom, the present managing director says, "My company stands or falls by its reputation for supplying excellent quality at competitive prices."

A Chelsea Gold Medal winner for 38 years in succession, Mr Blom offers a rich selection. This includes bulbs for all seasons, both indoors and out. The ornamental garlic, allium, and the autumn-flowering crocus, colchicum, particularly attracted me. They could add a new dimension to many Spanish gardens. If you want to own a very rare and beautiful specimen, consider the autumn crocus *Speciosum album,* whose large, white goblet flowers are filled with golden stamens.

Harkness, The Rose Gardens, Hitchin, Herts SG4 0JT, England. Tel. (0462) 420402. No minimum order. Shipping fee £8.50.

With this family firm (the five directors all bear the name Harkness) it is roses, roses all the way.

Their catalogue is a book of enchantment for all who love roses, and describes the 300 roses which they consider the loveliest in the world.

They urge you to buy collections as a way of saving money. If you feel uncertain what to choose, write in, and advice is gladly given. For the Harkness family, roses are more than just a way of making a living. They are a way of life.

Hilliers Nurseries, Ampfield House, Ampfield, Romsey, Hants SO5 9PA, England. Tel. (0794) 68733. No minimum order. Shipping cost £30.

This firm, which has won a Gold Medal at every Chelsea show for 40 years, offers in its catalogue, together with a brief description, about five thousand "woody" plants. Special emphasis is laid on fragrance in the garden.

The great advantage of these plants, very many of which are suitable for the Spanish climate, is that once safely in the soil they will live for years.

Suttons Seeds, Hele Road, Torquay, Devon TQ2 7QJ, England. Tel. (0803) 612011. Seeds only. Shipping fee £28.50, plus £10 postage and £10 for health certificate.

Suttons, who are now over a hundred years old, tell me that their illustrated catalogue takes a whole year to produce, and is followed by an avalanche of orders which arrive at the rate of 3,000 a day. The cheerful, young Flower Seed manager, explains that he checks strains of new varieties in many countries round the world and then has the best of them tested further at their trial grounds in Devon.

Seeds for a wealth of flowers are offered in this catalogue, as well as vegetables, both old favourites and newer introductions. From ornamental vegetables to herbs or patio tomatoes, there is something to interest every gardener — more seeds than one could grow in a happy lifetime.

Thompson and Morgan, London Road, Ipswich IP2 0BA, Suffolk, England. Tel. (0473) 688821; also, Dept. SS5, P.O. Box 1308, Jackson, New Jersey 08527, USA. Minimum order from England £12 plus postage.

Founded in 1885 and now operating on both sides of the Atlantic, Thompson and Morgan have a reputation for bold and adventurous introductions. This was the firm to which Charles Darwin sent back botanical material from his expeditions, and to which "Chinese" Wilson brought the results of his intrepid journeys into the interior of China.

Keith Sangster, the British chairman, heads a group which probably lists more novel and unusual seeds than any other supplier. You want to raise your own water-lilies, grow Californian wild flowers or West Indian holly? Thompson and Morgan have the seeds.

The illustrated colour catalogue contains 220 pages of information and compulsive reading.

Van Tubergen UK Ltd, Bressingham, Diss, Norfolk IP22 2AB, England. Tel. (0379) 888282.

Part of the Dutch firm of the same name, this company could probably claim to be the greatest bulb grower in the world and offers a wide range of popular and also uncommon bulbs.

I once had the good fortune to see some of their ancestral photographs, showing small, brown tents, pitched long ago beyond the Caspian sea, as their pioneer bulb collectors went about their business.

Today their collection includes many bulbs suited to the Spanish climate, such as the Paperwhite and very many other types of narcissus. Other beautiful flowers, like the amarine with its deep pink blooms (very long-lasting in water), or the veltheimia from South Africa, may be less familiar but are certainly welcome.

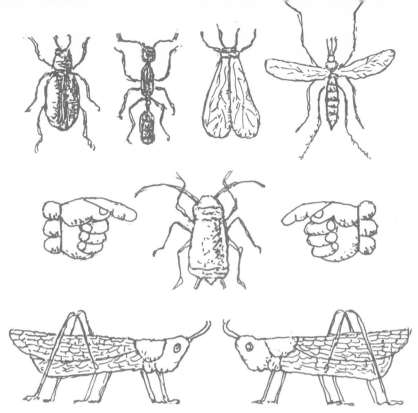

Garden Pests and How To Deal with Them

BUGS in the garden — a thought distasteful to every gardener, conjuring up visions of beautiful flowers destroyed by silent enemies.

Yet many insects in our gardens are beneficial, doing more good than harm. Nature has its own checks and balances. Indiscriminate chemical warfare puts an end not only to plant enemies but also to butterflies, honey-bees and other benign creatures such as ladybirds, lace wings and praying mantis. (If you want to increase your stock of praying mantis, look out for the nests when walking in the country. They are brown and wrinkled, rather like a walnut, and are likely to be found on trees.) Chemicals also banish wild birds which are forced to look for a living elsewhere.

A Policy to Control Pests

Garden pests are far more likely to attack any plant that is under stress and not totally happy with its environment. Minimize risk by growing plants that do well in your area.

First Try Non-Toxic Remedies

Some insects such as mites — tiny, eight-legged insects that look like red, yellow or green specks and harm plants by sucking the sap — flourish in the dust that gathers on garden plants in hot weather.

Water the whole plant with a rose on the hose-pipe as well as giving water to the roots. Greenfly can be controlled in the same way. Follow up with a spray of soap solution to kill any that have not been washed away. Diluted Green Fairy Liquid is ideal as it is a pure soap solution. If that isn't available, make your own solution with soap and water. Apply with a hand spray.

Manual Control

Catch and destroy snails and caterpillars by hand, or plant marigolds which are said to deter them. One flower gardener told me, "Marigolds are good for everything," and planted rows of marigolds throughout his patch. Scientists today tell us that the roots of marigolds secrete beneficial substances into the soil.

Another form of manual control is to watch over your garden and catch any infestation before it has time to spread. If blight appears on part of an orange tree, for instance, amputate and burn the branch. Much can be done by vigilance.

When Vigilance is Not Enough

Keen as many gardeners are to preserve the environment, sometimes all-out warfare is needed. This is the case with the very large mole cricket. Fortunately these predators are not common and usually infest gardens out in the country. They make holes about 2 cm. in diameter and are almost impossible to dig out as the holes go down about one metre. They feed on the roots of plants and so kill them, and actually draw down seedlings and eat them below the surface of the ground. Kill mole crickets with "Dipterex", manufactured in Spain by Bayer Hispania. Apply down the holes in accordance with the directions supplied. With all insecticides read instructions carefully and follow them to the letter.

"Roseclear" manufactured by ICI (Imperial Chemical Industries) of England combines fungicides with systemic insecticides. A systemic insecticide permeates the whole plant and so kills any predator feeding on it.

Use "Roseclear" on all plants in the garden, not only on roses. It will kill greenfly and aphids and any other pest which feeds on the leaves or sucks the sap of the plant, and leave untouched ladybirds, lacewings and bees.

"Pokon" plant spray from Holland, Murphy's "Tumblebug" made in England and Bayer's "Croneton" and "Lizetan" are among good chemical products usually available in Spain which kill all foliar insect pests. Unfortunately, good insects may suffer as well as bad.

When using a spray pesticide, remember that more insects live under leaves than on top of them.

Special Protection for Vines

If you decide to use all-out chemical warfare to protect your climbing vine, Bayer Hispania have the strategy for you. It combines a programme of attack on parasites and fungal infection, plus foliar feeding to strengthen the vine and so make it better able to overcome problems.

Step 1: From pruning time to the coming of the first leaves, spray with "Folithion" (dilute 2cc per litre of water) to counteract pests. Be careful to spray the leaves well.

Step 2: When the shoots are 25 cm. long until the flower clusters are visible use the anti-fungicide "Euparen" (2g per litre of water) plus the foliar feed "Bayfolan S" (3cc per litre) and "Dipterex" (2.5cc per litre). The "Dipterex" is designed to catch the first generation of insects attacking the fruit buds and may be omitted if none appear.

Step 3: Immediately after flowering until two weeks before harvest, spray every two weeks with a mixture of "Euparen" mixed with "Bayfolan." If needed, spray with "Dipterex" to control the second and third generation of insects attacking the bunches of fruit. This treatment will also control fruit-fly. Use as soon as you see signs of the invaders. Not necessary otherwise.

In the event of an attack of red mite, spray with "Folithion". (Never mix "Folithion" with "Euparen".) Stop all treatment two weeks before picking the grapes.

Dealing With Flies and Mosquitoes

Some garden pests can trouble the gardener rather than the plants. If flies and mosquitoes are a nuisance, take the first step by dealing with possible breeding grounds.

If your house is covered with creepers, strip the walls bare. This often results in a marked decrease in the fly population.

Mosquitoes breed in stagnant water, such as old, uncovered wells or still pools. The larvae must have oxygen. If you can reach the source of the trouble, float paraffin or other light oil over the surface, and the mosquito larvae will perish.

Remove any fly-attracting plants, such as the flowering succulent stapelia (whose exotic flowers smell of rotting meat and attract — and are fertilized by — flies).

Plants that Deter Flies

In Spain the elderberry bush or the herb basil are often grown round the doors of houses to keep flies away.

White jasmine with its sweet scent also has the reputation of deterring the flying insect population, as does the attractive *dama de noche,* lady of the night *(Cestrum nocturnum).* It releases its delightful perfume after dark when some of the most troublesome mosquitoes are on the wing. This plant has no popular English name.

The eau-de-cologne mint, *Mentha x piperita citrata* (give the full name if you order from a specialist nursery, it will help them to supply exactly what you want), is another aromatic plant with a reputation for driving flies away.

A most interesting suggestion was made to me by A.J. Halstead, one of Britain's leading entomologists. Many of us have used oil of citronella to keep off insects when gardening. Mr Halstead suggests that flies can be controlled by growing the Asian grass from which the oil is extracted.

In the past there has been confusion between "lemon grass", a herb used in Asian cooking which grows well in Spain, and the citronella grass used commercially for the extraction of citronella oil. Hunt for this grass from India and Sri Lanka under its botanical name *Cymbopogon nardus.*

It is probable that the seed can be obtained from two Indian firms of seed merchants (you can write in English). Try: Pratrap Nursery and Seed Stores, P.O. Pramnagar, Dehra Dun — 6, Goregaon, Bombay — 6z, India. Or: Jaya Pritam Lal, 15A 58 Diddharrhuagar, Goregaon, Bombay — 6z.

Pioneering gardeners — and there are many in Spain — may well find this scented oil grass the answer to the problem of flies and mosquitoes.

A Gardener's Almanac

 VERY new year brings fresh possibilities in the garden. A new lawn perhaps; new trees and shrubs, or a greater profusion of flowers and vegetables than ever before. Here is what you can do each month to turn ideas into reality.

JANUARY A major month for planting hedges, trees, bushes and climbers. Stake slender trees firmly.

Cut back now any roses not yet pruned.

Prune bougainvillaea hard. Prune hibiscus and jasmine more gently, also lantana, plumbago and other shrubs and climbers. Cut back poinsettia stems as the bushes become untidy. If not too much of an eyesore, leave for another 6-8 weeks to allow the sap to return to the main root-stock and strengthen the plant.

Last chance for pruning wistaria.

Take hard-wood cuttings of bougainvillaea.

Repot hippeastrum (amaryllis) bulbs which have flowered at Christmas.

Top-dress fine lawns with sand and peat.

Plant early potatoes, cabbage, cauliflower, broad beans, garlic, lettuce, radishes and tomatoes.

FEBRUARY can be the wettest and windiest month in the year.

Check that your garden is protected. If necessary plan wind-breaks in the form of trees, hedges or walls.

Plant trees and shrubs, staking well.

Plant lilies, begonias, dahlias and gladioli.

Make a first sowing of annuals such as nasturtium and sunflower, honesty, candytuft, godetia and clarkia.

Sowings may be repeated throughout the spring.

Plant out herbacious perennials if not done in autumn.

Some, such as pyrethrum and gaillardia do particularly well from a spring sowing.

Take cuttings of pinks and geraniums.

Sow cabbage, cauliflower, beetroot, silver-beet (Swiss chard), broad beans, carrots, leeks, lettuce, onions, peas, spinach and tomatoes.

MARCH See that the flower-beds are hoed, tidy and with neat edges.

Lawns need regular mowing from now on.

A good month for making a new lawn.

Start the summer watering routine as needed.

Plant bulbs and tubers for summer flowering, such as begonias, gladioli and tiger-lilies.

Plant water-lilies.

Sow biennials such as hollyhocks (which will almost certainly reseed themselves) and Sweet William. Plant catmint, coreopsis and gaillardia.

Make a planting of pinks to flower later in the summer.

Top-dress lawns with compound fertilizer. If there is no rain, water well.

Sow nemesia, gazania, arctotis (don't over-water) and freesia now. Freesias grown from seed will often come into flower earlier next spring than those grown from bulbs.

Give citrus — and other trees — an application of sulphate of ammonia.

In the vegetable garden sow aubergine, beetroot, cabbage, carrots, cauliflower, cucumber, French beans, leeks, lettuce, melon, pumpkin and silver-beet.

APRIL Propagate Christmas cactus by cuttings inserted 7 cm. in sandy soil.

Another good month to sow biennials. Consider new plantings of coreopsis, freesia, gaillardia, lobelia and zinnia.

Plant more bulbs and tubers for summer flowering such as gladioli, begonias and tiger-lilies.

Check on newly-planted roses to see that they are firm in the soil after the spring winds. Tread in if necessary.

Repot citrus trees in containers when needed, as soon as they have made their new growth. If repotting is not necessary, give a top dressing of peaty compost.

Another good month for making new lawns.

In the kitchen garden sow aubergine, beetroot, cabbage, cauliflower, carrots, French beans, leeks, lettuce, melon, water-melon and silver-beet.

Keep all plants well watered and weed-free.

MAY The flower garden is in full colour now. Keep down incipient weeds and aerate soil by regular hoeing.

Keep up watering and mowing routines.

Dead-head flowers promptly to encourage new bloom. Roses, sweet-peas and antirrhinums respond particularly well.

Plant out Sweet William and other biennials as the seedlings grow large enough to handle, either this month or next.

Give cannas a dose of weak liquid manure.

Cut back flowering shrubs throughout the summer as bloom finishes.

Take cuttings of busy Lizzie and put small shoots in water until fine roots form, then pot up.

Propagate the flowering climbers allemanda and streptosolen by taking 8-cm. cuttings of lateral shoots and planting in sandy soil.

Increase irises by lifting bulbs or rhizomes immediately after flowering. Sea lavender blooms from now on according to the position of the garden. Cut and hang up to dry for winter.

Sow beetroot, cabbage, cauliflower, French beans, leeks, silver-beet and tomatoes.

JUNE Another month when gardens are at their best. Day-lilies, cat-mint, roses, African lilies, delphiniums, geraniums. Pride of Peru and perfumed pinks are all blazing away.

Keep up regular watering. Although early morning and evening are ideal times, the use of sprinklers all day reduces work and is adequate for all but the most delicate plants.

Where water is scarce or expensive, perforated plastic tubing will deliver it just where it is needed in regulated amounts.

Mow lawns regularly. Little and often produces better results than the occasional close shave.

Keep up the dead-heading. Go over rose-bushes daily for best results.

Continue to prune flowering shrubs as soon as the blossom fades.

Cut back shoots that have bloomed to good side-shoots or outward-growing buds.

Propagate philadelphus now by inserting young shoots in sandy soil.

Check that the compost heap does not dry out.

Make successional sowings of cabbage, carrots, cauliflower, French beans, leeks, silver-beet and tomatoes.

JULY Watering is the main job this month.

Mimosa, datura, lantana and bougainvillaea are in the middle of their long flowering season.

Keep roses and all flowers dead-headed for maximum blooom.

Now that the soil is really warm, cuttings of pride of Madeira (echium) do well if protected from strong sunlight.

Make a first sowing of blazing star (liatris), calendula, heliotrope and pansies for next year.

Clip yew hedges and bushes.

In the kitchen garden reap where you have sown. As spent crops are cleared away, manure the ground well and sow cabbage, carrots, cauliflower, French beans and silver-beet for the winter.

AUGUST Watering, mowing and dead-heading are the main jobs now.

Take cuttings of oleander and hibiscus.

Late in the month sow stocks, antirrhinums, pansies and verbena. Continue to hoe regularly to keep down weeds and aerate the soil. This prevents cracking and the consequent loss of moisture.

Pay particular attention to the deep watering of any young trees not yet fully established. Shallow watering causes the roots to turn upwards and hinders the formation of a sound root structure.

Plant Madonna lilies.

Sow cabbage, carrots, cauliflower, leeks, lettuce, onions and potatoes.

SEPTEMBER If more compost is needed than can be made from normal kitchen and garden waste, arrange to buy extra supplies of organic material. Spent mushroom compost is useful. Clear away spent annuals and biennials.

Cut back petunias, phlox and lobelia when flowering is over.

They will often spring up again.

Take cuttings of deciduous trees and shrubs.

In the kitchen garden sow for the winter cabbage, carrots, cauliflower, leeks, lettuce, onions and silver-beet.

OCTOBER is a month of great opportunity in the garden. The soil is in ideal condition for most types of planting.

Put in shrubs and roses. Remove any suckers from existing roses.

Prepare new herbacious borders now.

Plant out antirrhinums, petunias, verbena and stocks.

Clear away any remaining spent annuals.

Towards the end of the month start ripe-wood cuttings of shrubs.

Plant new lawns.

Take cuttings of geraniums and root-cuttings of other perennials.

Some gardeners like to sow sweet peas now to get them off to a good start next spring.

Propagate asparagus fern by root-cuttings.

Plant out seedlings sown in August of antirrhinums, pansies, stocks and verbena.

Sow broad beans, cabbage, carrots, cauliflower, endive, leeks, peas, tomatoes and silver-beet.

Prune oleander and other shrubs which have finished flowering.

NOVEMBER A good month for planting trees, hedges and shrubs.
Check that the garden is tidy and weed-free.
Start any necessary pruning of trees and shrubs, starting with olives and figs.
Plant bulbs for spring flowering, such as crocuses, daffodils, tulips, hyacinths and gladioli.
Broad beans, cabbage, carrots, cauliflower, lettuce, peas and silver-beat can still be sown.

DECEMBER Prune late-flowering shrubs such as buddleia and datura.
Last chance to plant tulips.
Thin and re-tie climbing roses.
Prune rose-bushes.
Remove water-shoots from bougainvillaea.
Cut out dead wood from citrus, as new growth is made early in the coming year.
Mulch young trees with manure or compost.
Sow broad beans, carrots, cabbage, cauliflower, French beans, garlic, leeks, peas, potatoes and silver-beet.

Vocabulary

ENGLISH-SPANISH

ACACIA: acacia
Acorus: acoro
Aeonium: eonio
African Hemp:
  esparmania
African Lily: agapanto
African Violet: violeta
  africana
Agapanthus: agapanto
Agave: pita; agave
Ageratum: agerato
Almond tree: almendro
Aloe: áloe
Aluminium Plant:
  madreperla
Alyssum: aliso
Amaranthus: amaranto
Amaryllis: amarilis
Anemone: anémona;
  coronaria
Angel's Trumpet:
  estramonio
Angelica: angélica
Antirrhinum: boca de
  dragón
Apple tree: manzano
Apricot tree:
  albaricoquero
Aquilegia: aguileña
Arbor Vitae: tuya
Arbutus: madroño
Artichoke: alcachofa
Arum: cala
Ash: fresno
Asparagus: espárrago
Asparagus Fern:
  esparraguera
Aspidistra: aspidistra

Aubergine: berenjena
Autumn Crocus:
  cólquico
Avocado: aguacate
Azalea: azalea

BALM: toronjil
Bamboo: bambú
Basil: albahaca
Bay: laurel
Beetroot: remolacha
Begonia: begonia
Bell Flower: farolillo
Belladonna Lily:
  azucena rosa
Berberis: agracejo;
  berberis; berbero
Bignonia: bignonia
**Bird-of-Paradise
Flower**: estrilicia; ave
  del paraíso
Bird's Nest Fern:
  helecho nido de ave
Black-Eyed Susan: ojo
  de poeta
Blackberry bush:
  zarzamora
Blue Marguerite:
  felicia
Bluebell: escila
Borage: borraja
Boston Fern: nefrolepis
Bottle-Brush:
  escobillon; calistemon
Bougainvillaea:
  buganvilla
Box: boj; bujo
Brake: helecho temblon
Broad Bean: haba
Broom: escoba; escobon;

genista; retama;
  piorno; taulaga;
  aulaguilla
Brussels Sprout: col de
  Bruselas
Busy Lizzie: gliceria;
  miramelindo

CABBAGE: col
Cactus: cáctus
Calendula: maravilla;
  caléndula
California Poppy:
  amapola de California
Callistemon: escobillon;
  calistemon
Camomile: manzanilla
Candytuft: iberis;
  carraspique
Canna Lily: caña de
  Indias
Caraway: alcaravea
Carnation: clavel
Carob: algarrobo
Carpobrotus: uña de
  gato; flor de cuchillo
Carrot: zanahoria
Castor Oil Plant: ricino
Cauliflower: coliflor
Century Plant: pita;
  agave
Ceratonia: algarrobo
Cestrum Nocturnum:
  dama de noche
Chard: acelga
Chervil: perifollo
Chilli: pimiento de chile;
  pimentón
Chive: cebollino
Chlorophytum:
  clorofito

Cineraria Maritima: cineraria marítima
Cistus: jara; cisto; estepa; jaguarzo
Citrus: cítrico; agrio
Clarkia: clarquia
Clematis: clemátide; vidalba
Clementine: clementina
Clivia: clivia
Cobaea: cobea
Colchicum: cólquico
Comfrey: consuelda; consólida
Coral Tree: árbol del coral
Coreopsis: coreopsis
Coriander: cilantro
Cornflower: centaurea; aciano
Cortaderia: hierba de las Pampas
Cotinus: árbol de las pelucas
Courgette: calabacín
Crassula: crasula
Cress: berro; mastuerzo
Crocus: azafrán
Crocus Sativus: azafrán
Cucumber: pepino
Cumin: comino
Cup-of-Gold Vine: solandra
Cupressus: ciprés
Currant: grosella
Custard Apple: chirimoya
Cycas: cica
Cyclamen: ciclamen
Cyperus: paraguas
Cypress: ciprés

DAFFODIL: narciso
Dahlia: dalia
Daisy: margarita
Dandelion: diente de león
Datura: estramonio
Day Lily: lirio japonés; lirio de San Juan
Delphinium: espuela
Dieffenbachia: difenbaquia

Dill: eneldo
Dogwood: cornejo
Dumb Cane: difenbaquia

ECHIUM: masaroco
Eggplant: berenjena
Eichhornia: jacinto de agua
Elderberry: saúco
Elephant's Ear: oreja de elefante
Endive: achicoria; endibia
Epteride: helecho temblon
Erythrina: árbol del coral
Eucalyptus: eucalipto
Euphorbia: euforbia; espino de Cristo

FALSE PEPPER TREE; pimentero
Fennel: hinojo
Fern: helecho
Feverfew: matricaria
Ficus Elastica: ficus; planta del caucho
Fig tree: higuera
Firethorn: piracanto; espino de fuego
Flax: lino
Florence Fennel: hinojo florentino
Four O'Clock: dondiego de noche
Forget-Me-Not: miosotis
Freesia: fresia; africana
French Bean: judía verde
Fuchsia: fucsia

GAILLARDIA: gallardia
Garlic: ajo
Gazania: gazania
Geranium: geránio
Germander: camedrio
Gherkin: pepinillo
Ginger: jengibre
Gladiolus: gladiolo
Godetia: godecia

Gorse: aulaga
Gourd: calabaza de agua
Grama Grass: grama
Grape Hyacinth: nazareno
Grape Vine: parra
Grapefruit: pomelo
Guava: guayaba
Hebe: verónica

HELICHRYSUM: siempreviva
Herb: hierba aromática
Hibiscus: hibisco; rosa de China; rosa de Siria
Hippeastrum: amarilis
Holly: acebo
Hollyhock: malva real
Holm Oak: encina
Honesty: lunaria
Honeysuckle: madreselva
Horseradish: rábano rusticiano; rábano picante
Hyacinth: jacinto
Hydrangea: hortensia
Hyssop: hisopo

ICE-PLANT: uña de gato; flor de cuchillo
Ipomoea: ipomea; campanilla
Iris: lírio
Ivy: hiedra

JACARANDA: jacaranda
Jade Pant: crasula
Jasmine: jazmín
Jerusalem Artichoke: aguaturma; cotufa
Jonquil: jonquillo
Judas Tree: árbol del amor
Juniper: enebro

KAFFIR LILY: clivia minuta

LABURNUM: lluvia de oro
Land Cress: berro de jardin; mastuerzo

Lantana: lantana
Larkspur: espuela de caballero
Lavatera: lavatera
Lavender: espliego; lavanda; lavándula
Lavender Cotton: santolina
Leek: puerro
Leonotis: oreja de león
Lemon tree: limonero
Lemon Grass: hierba luisa
Lettuce: lechuga
Lily: lírio; azucena
Lily of the Nile: agapanto
Lime tree: limero
Limonium: siempreviva azul
Lion's Ear: oreja de leon
Lobelia: lobelia
Locust (Robinia): acacia
Loquat: níspero
Lotus: flor de loto
Lovage: levístico
Love-in-a-Mist: araña; neguilla de Damasco
Lunaria: lunaria

MADONNA LILY: lírio de San Antonio
Magnolia: magnolia
Maidenhair Fern: culantrillo
Malvaviscus: malvavisco
Mandarin: mandarina
Mandevilla: suspiros
Marigold: clavelón; clavel de moro; tagete; caléndula
Marjoram: mejorana
Marrow: calabacín
Melon: melón
Mentha Pulegium: poleo
Mignonette: reseda
Mimosa: mimosa
Mint: hierbabuena, menta
Mock Orange: celinda
Monstera Deliciosa: costilla de Adán

Morning Glory: campanilla; ipomea
Mother-in-law's Tongue: sanseveria
Myporum: transparente
Myrrh: mirra; opobálsamo
Myrtle: arrayán

NARCISSUS: narciso
Nasturtium: capuchina
Neoregelia: neoregelia
Nephrolepis: nefrolepis
Night Jasmine: dama de noche

OAK: roble; encina; alcornoque
Oleander: adelfa
Olive tree: olivo
Onion: cebolla
Orange tree: naranjo
Oregano: orégano

PALM: palmera
Pampas-Grass: hierba de las Pampas
Pansy: pensamiento
Papaw: papaya
Parsley: perejíl
Parsnip: chirivia
Passion Flower: pasionaria
Pea: guisante
Pear tree: peral
Pennyroyal: poleo
Peperomia: peperomia
Pepper: pimiento
Pepper Tree: pimentero
Periwinkle: vincapervinca
Petunia: petunia
Philadelphus: celinda
Phlox: Flox
Pilea: madreperla
Pine: pino
Pink: clavellina; clavelillo
Pittosporum: pitosporo; azahar de China
Plane Tree: platano
Plum tree: ciruelo
Plum Tomato: tomate de pera

Plumbago: celestina; jazmín azúl
Poinsettia: pascuero; flor de pascua
Pomegranate tree: granado
Poppy: amapola; adormidera
Portulaca: verdolaga
Potato: patata
Prickly Pear: chumbera
Pride of Madeira: masaroco
Pumpkin: calabaza
Pyracantha: piracanto; espino de fuego

QUINCE: membrillo

RADISH: rábano
Raspberry: frambueso
Robinia: acacia
Rock-Rose: jara; cisto; estepa; jaguarzo
Rose bush: rosal
Rosemary: romero
Rubber Plant: ficus; planta del caucho
Runner Bean: judía pinta
Russelia: lágrimas de amor

SAFFRON: azafrán
Sage: salvia
Sagitarria: sagitaria
Sago Palm: cica
Salad Burnet: sanguisorba
Salvia: salvia
Sansevieria: sanseviera
Schinus: pimentero
Sea-Daffodil: azucena de mar; nebulosa
Sea Lavender: siempreviva azul
Selaginella: selaginela
Sesame: ajonjolí; sésamo
Silver-Beet: acelga
Smoke Tree: árbol de las pelucas
Snapdragon: boca de dragón

Snow Pea: guisante de Tribeque
Solandra: solandra
Solanum: solano
Sorrel: acedera
Sparmannia: esparmania
Spider Plant: cinta; clorofito
Spinach: espinaca
Spiraea: espirea
Staghorn Fern: cuerno de ciervo
Stock: alhelí
Strawberry: fresal; fresa
Strawberry Tree: madroño
Strawflower: siempreviva
Strelitzia: estrilicia; ave del paraíso
Summer Savory: ajedrea blanca

Sunflower: girasol
Sweet Corn: maíz dulce
Sweet Flag: acoro
Sweet Pea: guisante de olor
Sweet Pepper: pimiento
Sweet Potato: boniato; batata
Sweet William: minutisa
Swiss Chard: acelga

TAMARISK: tamarisco
Tarragon: estragón
Taxus: tejo
Teucrium: camedrio
Thuya: tuya
Thyme: tomillo
Tiger-Lily: lirio tigrado
Tobacco Plant: nicotiana
Tomato vine: tomatera
Tulip: tulipán

UMBRELLA PLANT: paraguas

VENETIAN SUMACH: árbol de las pelucas
Verbena: verbena
Violet: violeta

WATER HYACINTH: jacinto de agua
Water Lily: nenúfar
Watermelon: sandia
Winter Savory: ajedrea común; sejalida
Wistaria: wisteria; glicina

YEW: tejo
Yucca: yuca

ZANTEDESCHIA: cala
Zinnia: zinia
Zucchini: calabacín

SPANISH-ENGLISH

ACACIA: acacia; locust (robinia)
Acebo: holly
Acedera: sorrel
Acelga: chard; silver-beet
Achicoria: endive
Aciano: cornflower
Acoro: sweet flag
Adelfa: oleander
Adormidera: poppy
Agapanto: agapanthus
Agave: agave; century plant
Agerato: ageratum
Aguacate: avocado
Aguileña: aquilegia
Agracejo: berberis
Aguaturma: Jerusalem artichoke
Ajedrea blanca: summer savory

Ajedrea común: winter savory
Ajo: garlic
Ajonjolí: sesame
Albahaca: basil
Albaricoquero: apricot tree
Alcachofa: artichoke
Alcaravea: caraway
Alcornoque: cork-oak
Algarrobo: carob tree
Alhelí: stock
Aliso: allysum
Almendro: almond tree
Aloe: aloe
Amapola: poppy
Amaranto: amaranthus
Amarilis: amaryllis
Anémona: anemone
Angélica: angelica
Aulaga: gorse
Aulaguilla: broom
Ave del paraíso: bird-of-paradise flower;

strelitzia
Araña: love-in-a-mist
Arbol de las pelucas: smoke tree; cotinus
Arbol del amor: Judas tree
Arbol del coral: coral tree; erythrina
Arrayán: myrtle
Aspidistra: aspidistra
Azafrán: saffron; crocus
Azahar de China: pittosporum
Azucena: lily
Azucena rosa: belladonna lily

BAMBU: bamboo
Batata: sweet potato
Begonia: begonia
Berbero: berberis
Berenjena: aubergine; eggplant
Bignonia: bignonia

Berro: cress; watercress
Berro de jardín:
land-cress
Boca de dragón:
snapdragon;
antirrhinum
Boj: box
Boniato: sweet potato
Borraja: borage
Buganvilla:
bougainvillaea
Bujo: box

CACTUS: cáctus
Cala: arum;
zantedeschia
Calabacín: courgette;
marrow; zucchini
Calabaza: pumpkin
Calabaza de agua:
gourd
Caléndula: calendula;
marigold
Calistemon:
bottle-brush
Camedrio: germander;
teucrium
Campanilla: morning
glory; ipomoea
Caña de Indias: canna
lily
Capuchina: nasturtium
Carraspique: candytuft
Cebolla: onion
Cebollino: chive
Celestina: plumbago
Celinda: mock orange;
philadelphus
Centaurea: cornflower
Chirimoya: custard
apple
Chirivia: parsnip
Chumbera: prickly pear
Cica: sago palm; cycas
Ciclamen: cyclamen
Cilantro: coriander
Cinta: spider plant
Ciprés: cypress;
cupressus
Ciruelo: plum tree
Cisto: cistus; rock-rose
Clarquia: clarkia
Clavel: carnation
Clavel de moro:

marigold
Clavelillo: pink
Clavellina: pink
Clavelón: marigold
Clematide: clematis
Clementina: clementine
Clivia: clivia
Clorofito: spider plant;
chlorophytum
Cobea: Cobaea
Col: cabbage
Col de Bruselas:
Brussels sprout
Coliflor: cauliflower
Cólquico: colchicum;
autumn crocus
Comino: cumin
Consólida: comfrey
Consuelda: comfrey
Coreopsis: coreopsis
Cornejo: dogwood
Coronaria: anemone
Costilla de Adan:
monstera
Cotufa: Jerusalem
artichoke
Crasula: jade plant;
crassula
Cuerno de ciervo:
staghorn fern
Culantrillo: maidenhair
fern

DALIA: dahlia
Dama de noche:
cestrum nocturnum;
night jasmine
Diente de leon:
dandelion
Difenbaquia:
dieffenbachia; dumb
cane
Dondiego de noche:
four o'clock

ENCINA: holm-oak
Endibia: endive
Enebro: juniper
Eneldo: dill
Eonio: aeonium
Escila: bluebell
Escoba: broom
Escobillon:
bottle-brush;

callistemon
Escobon: broom
Espárrago: asparagus
Esparraguera:
asparagus fern
Espinaca: spinach
Espino de Cristo:
euphorbia
Espino de fuego:
firethorn
Espirea: spiraea
Espliego: lavender
Espuela: delphinium
Espuela de caballero:
larkspur
Estepa: cistus; rock-rose
Estragón: tarragon
Estramonio: datura;
angel's trumpet
Estrilicia:
bird-of-paradise flower;
strelitzia
Eucalipto: eucalyptus
Euforbia: euphorbia

FAROLILLO: bell
flower
Felicia: blue marguerite
Ficus: ficus; rubber
plant
Flor de cuchillo:
carpobrotus; ice-plant
Flor de loto: lotus
Flor de pascua:
poinsettia
Flox: phlox
Frambueso: raspberry
Fresa: strawberry
Fresno: ash
Fucsia: fuchsia

GALLARDIA: gaillardia
Gazania: gazania
Genista: broom
Geranio: geranium
Girasol: sunflower
Gladiolo: gladiolus
Gliceria: busy Lizzie
Glicina: wistaria
Godecia: godetia
Granado: pomegranate
Grosella: currant
Guayaba: guava
Guisante: pea

Guisante de olor: sweet pea
Guisante de tribeque: snow pea

HABA: broad bean
Helecho: fern
Helecho nido de pájaro: bird's nest fern
Helecho temblon: brake; epteride
Hibisco: hibiscus
Hiedra: ivy
Hierba de las Pampas: Pampas grass; cortaderia
Hierbabuena: mint
Hierbaluisa: lemon grass
Higuera: fig tree
Hinojo: fennel
Hisopo: hyssop
Hortensia: hydrangea

IBERIS: candytuft
Ipomea: morning glory; ipomoea

JACARANDA: jacaranda
Jacinto: hyacinth
Jacinto de agua: water hyacinth; eichhornia
Jaguarzo: cistus; rock-rose
Jara: cistus; rock-rose
Jazmín: jasmine
Jazmín azúl: plumbago
Jengibre: ginger
Jonquillo: jonquil
Judía: green bean; French bean

LAGRIMAS DE AMOR: russelia
Lantana: lantana
Laurel: bay
Lavanda: lavender
Lavandula: lavender
Lavatera: lavatera
Lechuga: lettuce
Levístico: lovage
Limero: lime tree
Limonero: lemon tree

Lino: flax
Lirio: lily; iris
Lirio de san Juan: day lily
Lirio japonés: day lily
Lluvia de oro: laburnum
Lobelia: lobelia
Lunaria: honesty; lunaria

MADREPERLA: aluminium plant; pilea
Madreselva: honeysuckle
Madroño: arbutus; strawberry tree
Magnolia: magnolia
Maíz dulce: sweet corn
Malva real: hollyhock
Mandarina: mandarin
Manzanilla: camomile
Manzano: apple tree
Margarita: daisy
Masaroco: pride of Madeira; echium
Mastuerzo: land-cress
Matricaria: feverfew
Mejorana: marjoram
Melón: melon
Membrillo: quince
Menta: mint
Mimosa: mimosa
Minutisa: sweet william
Miosotis: forget-me-not
Miramelindo: busy Lizzie
Mirra: myrrh

NARANJO: orange tree
Narciso: narcissus; daffodil
Nazareno: grape hyacinth
Nebulosa: sea-daffodil
Nefrolepis: Boston fern; nephrolepis
Neguilla de Damasco: love-in-a-mist
Nenúfar: water-lily
Neoregelia: neoregelia
Nicotiana: tobacco plant
Níspero: loquat

OJO DE POETA: black-eyed Susan
Olivo: olive tree
Opobálsamo: myrrh
Orégano: oregano
Oreja de leon: lion's ear; leonotis
Orejas de elefante: elephant's ears

PALMERA: palm tree
Papaya: papaw
Paraguas: cyperus; umbrella plant
Parra: grape vine
Pascuero: poinsettia
Patata: potato
Pasionaria: passion flower
Pensamiento: pansy
Peperomia: peperomia
Pepinillo: gherkin
Pepino: cucumber
Peral: pear tree
Perejíl: parsley
Perifollo: chervil
Petunia: petunia
Pimentero: pepper tree; schinus
Pimentón: chilli
Pimiento: pepper
Pimiento de Chile: chilli
Pino: pine
Piorno: broom
Piracanto: firethorn; pyracanthus
Pita: agave; century plant
Pitosporo: pittosporum
Planta de caucho: rubber plant
Platano: plane tree
Poleo: pennyroyal; mentha pulegium
Pomelo: grapefruit
Puerro: leek

RABANO: radish
Rábano rusticiano: horseradish
Remolacha: beetroot
Reseda: mignonette
Retama: broom

Ricino: castor oil plant
Roble: oak
Romero: rosemary
Rosa: rose
Rosal: rose bush

SAGITARIA: sagittaria
Salvia: sage; salvia
Sandía: watermelon
Sanguisorba: salad
  burnet
Sanseveria:
  sansevieria;
  mother-in-law's tongue
Santolina: lavender
  cotton
Sauco: elderberry
Sejalida: winter savory
Selaginela: selaginella
Sésamo: sesame
Siempreviva:

strawflower;
  helichrysum; sea
  lavender;
  limonium
Solandra: cup-of-gold
  vine; solandra
Solano: solanum
Suspiros: mandevilla

TAGETE: marigold
Tamarisco: tamarisk
Taulaga: broom
Tejo: yew; taxus
Tomate: tomato
Tomate de pera: plum
  tomato
Tomatera: tomato vine
Tomillo: thyme
Toronjíl: balm
Tulipan: tulip
Tuya: thuya; arbor vitae

UÑA DE GATO:
  carpobrotus; ice-plant

VERBENA: verbena
Verdolaga: portulaca
Verónica: hebe
Vidalba: clematis
Vincapervinca:
  periwinkle
Violeta: violet
Violeta africana:
  African violet

WISTERIA: wistaria

YUCA: yucca

ZANAHORIA: carrot
Zarzamora: blackberry
  vine
Zinia: zinnia

Index of Plants

For a full list of our
essential books on Spain contact:
Santana Books,
Apartado 422,
29640 Fuengirola (Málaga) Spain.
Tel: 952 485 838. Fax: 952 485 367.
E-mail: sales@santanabooks.com
website: www.santanabooks.com

UK Representatives
Aldington Books Ltd.,
Unit 3(b) Frith Business Centre,
Frith Road, Aldington,
Ashford, Kent TN25 7HJ.
Tel: 01233 720 123. Fax: 01233 721 272
E-mail: sales@aldingtonbooks.co.uk
www.aldingtonbooks.co.uk

CONVERSION TABLES

LENGTH

Centimetres		Inches	Inches		Centimetres
1	=	½	1	=	2.5
5	=	2	3	=	7.5
10	=	4	6	=	15
15	=	6	9	=	22.5
25	=	10	12	=	30.5
50	=	20	18	=	45.5
75	=	30	24	=	61
100	=	39	36	=	91.5

TEMPERATURE

Centigrade		Fahrenheit
0	=	32
5	=	41
10	=	50
15	=	59
20	=	68
25	=	77
30	=	86
35	=	93
40	=	104
45	=	113
50	=	122